Second Edition

MORE than **50** **Ways to**

BUILD

Team Consensus

MORE than 50 Ways to BUILD Team Consensus

Second Edition

R. Bruce Williams

CORWIN PRESS
A SAGE Publications Company
Thousand Oaks, California

For information:

Corwin Press, Inc.
A Sage Publications Company
2455 Teller Road
Thousand Oaks, California 91320
www.corwinpress.com

Sage Publications Ltd.
1 Oliver's Yard
55 City Road
London EC1Y 1SP
United Kingdom

Sage Publications India Pvt. Ltd.
B-42, Panchsheel Enclave
Post Box 4109
New Delhi 110 017 India

Printed in the United States of America.

This book is printed on acid-free paper.

Library of Congress Cataloging-in-Publication Data

Williams, R. Bruce.
More than 50 ways to build team consensus / R. Bruce Williams.—2nd ed.
    p. cm.
Includes bibliographical references and index.
ISBN 1-4129-3710-8 (cloth)—ISBN 1-4129-3711-6 (pbk.)
    1. Teams in the workplace. 2. Group decision making. 3. Consensus (Social Sciences) I. Title: More than fifty ways to build team consensus. II. Title.

HD66.W54 2007
658.4'022—dc22   2006005420

06 07 08 09 10 10 9 8 7 6 5 4 3 2 1

Acquisitions Editor:	Cathy Hernandez
Editorial Assistant:	Charline Wu
Project Editor:	Kate Peterson
Copy Editor:	Bonnie Freeman
Typesetter:	C&M Digitals (P) Ltd.
Indexer:	Pamela Van Huss
Cover Designer:	Scott Van Atta

Contents

Preface

A dramatic change has occurred in today's workplace. Many people are being called on to manage through teams. To work through teams, we need tools and strategies to facilitate consensus as never before. There are no easy, clearcut models to move an organization from top-down, hierarchical decision making to team decisions based on consensus. Consensus tools are needed so that organizations can move into this uncharted territory with confidence.

When these tools and strategies are used to create a purposeful vision, encourage participative processes, enhance individual commitment, and build a collaborative team, consensus can begin to grow. Shortchange any one of these components, and the consensus is lopsided or incomplete. Without a vision, there is no focus to a consensus and no reason for one. Without participative processes, there is no road map for the group to follow through the intricacies of building consensus meeting after meeting. Without individual commitment, there is no drive or energy to carry consensus through to completion. Finally, without a unified team, the task of consensus is overwhelming and burdensome. People burn out before consensus is reached.

Building consensus is not an overnight task. It is a process that takes years and can be refined year after year. Nevertheless, you can begin today with your team to set the stage for consensus to grow and to establish an environment that fosters consensus. As you mix tools and strategies from each section of this book, you will create a unique blend of approaches that will move your group toward trust and deep consensus.

Anyone interested in consensus may take this book and read it from cover to cover to gain a full grasp of the consensus process and a multitude of ways to generate consensus in a team. It is also possible to thumb through to an activity whose title seems interesting and just jump in and use it.

You may also choose strategies at simple, intermediate, or challenging levels. If your group has just come together for the first time or if your team is newly constituted, it might be helpful to delve into the strategies called Simple Things to Do. If your team has already worked together for several months and performs well, with perhaps just a few snags, see whether some of the medium-level strategies (Things That Take Effort) fit your situation. Teams that have been functioning well for quite a while may find that some of the more demanding strategies (For the Committed) help them build on their strengths.

This book is also organized into the four components of full consensus: Purposeful Vision, Participative Processes, Individual Commitment, and Collaborative Teams. Perhaps your team is manifesting signs that it needs some of the strategies associated with only one of the four major parts of this book. If your team is mired in the day-to-day, plodding tasks of implementation, some of the strategies of Purposeful Vision may help reinstate the team's awareness of the big picture and revive some of the energy shown in the team's early days.

If your team is argumentative and full of hassling, some of the strategies in Participative Processes may help channel and focus some of your team's energies. Furthermore, if one or two people are dominating your meetings, this section might be particularly useful.

When you find signs that your team or many individuals on your team are refusing responsibility or allowing only one or two people to do all the work, then your team might be assisted greatly by some of the strategies in Individual Commitment.

Last, if your team has strong-willed, competent individuals all pouring much energy into the task but rarely working together, explore the strategies in Collaborative Teams. Our culture has long encouraged strong individual action, often to the neglect of teamwork.

For a review of the theory and research behind some of the concepts represented in this book, please read the introductions to each part. These introductions summarize what other experts and practitioners are saying about consensus. The quotations at the beginning of each activity reinforce themes of the whole section.

Needless to say, if an activity does not appear to make any sense for your team at this time, go on to the next one and keep going until you find one that clicks with you and your team. Or if a strategy makes great sense to you but does not go over with the team, go on to another activity until you find one that works for all of you. Some of the activities are ones you do directly with your group. Others help you both before and after your meetings.

You might find it helpful, after you try something, to spend time thinking about what went well, exactly how people felt about what you did, why you think it went well, and how you might improve it the next time you use it. This kind of review and debriefing of yourself can strengthen your capacity and confidence as a facilitator.

After you try something suggested in this book, I would be delighted to hear how it worked for you. As you use these strategies, you may be building teams in places where very few teams have operated before. You are laying tracks for a whole new way of working. Let me know what worked, how well it worked, whether it flopped, and how you have improved activities.

Acknowledgments

For twenty years, my skills in group facilitation were honed by colleagues on the staff of the Institute of Cultural Affairs (ICA). Our daily use of participatory, consensus-building methods both internally and externally helped each of us deepen our attentiveness to the skills and styles that foster group connections. Some of ICA's wisdom in facilitation processes is contained in the book *Winning Through Participation*, by Laura Spencer, which is quoted numerous times in this book. Some of the activities described in this book came directly from my experiences with ICA. Others were certainly inspired by my work and training there.

I am grateful for all those who have made use of this book and found ways to let me know that it has been helpful to them. It has been encouraging to me that people in education, business, and not-for-profit organizations have discovered this book to be a valuable resource.

Family and countless friends have patiently followed and enabled the evolution of this book. Jack, Richard, Jim, and John have surrounded me with support and care that never stops.

PUBLISHER'S ACKNOWLEDGMENTS

Corwin Press gratefully acknowledges the contributions of the following reviewers:

Judith Allen Brough, Professor and Chair, Department of Education
Gettysburg College, Gettysburg, PA

Marta Ann Gardner, Literacy Coach
Esperanza Elementary School, Los Angeles, CA

Toni Jones, Principal
Deer Creek Middle School, Edmond, OK

Teresa Poulin Kane, Seventh- and Eighth-Grade Teacher
Warsaw Middle School, Pittsfield, ME

Stephen M. Laub, Principal
Rolla Junior High School, Rolla, MO

About the Author

 With more than thirty-five years of international consulting experience, Bruce Williams is noted for his expert group facilitation and his skills in planning and team-building methodologies. He has authored *Twelve Roles of Facilitators for School Change* and *36 Tools for Building Spirit in Learning Communities,* published by Corwin Press. He is the coauthor of *Valuing Diversity in the School System* and *Brain-Compatible Learning for the Block,* also published by Corwin Press. He recently released *Cooperative Learning: A Standard for High Achievement, Multiple Intelligences for Differentiated Learning,* and *Higher Order Thinking Skills: Challenging All Students to Achieve,* all published by Robin Fogarty and Associates. His specialty is facilitating participative, interactive group workshops, whether focused on strategic planning and consensus building or instructional methodologies for the classroom. Recently, his workshops titled Brain Compatible Learning and School Change Facilitation have been popular. In addition, he frequently presents in the areas of cooperative learning, higher order thinking skills, and authentic assessment.

Bruce's exceptional skill at dealing with diverse populations is aided by his seven years' experience in Japan and Korea teaching English as a second language. His thirty-six years of experience in adult training have enabled him to be an invaluable resource in facilitating school change.

In addition to conference workshops in 2002 in Australia and New Zealand, he has been invited three times to present workshops for teachers in Singapore. In April 2004, Bruce was the keynote speaker for 400 principals and teachers in Beijing, People's Republic of China.

Introduction to Building Team Consensus

To set the stage for the new edition of this book, I would like to summarize some of the insights that have emerged in the last decade in three crucial areas. The first is the area of brain research. This research has illuminated our understanding about how the brain works best and how to capitalize on its workings. Needless to say, this research has implications for education. It also has immense implications for leadership. Consequently, the second area focuses on recent thinking about effective leadership. Finally, given the rising demand for consensus processes, the third area is consensus itself.

THE BRAIN RESEARCH

Brain researchers identify three distinct sections of the brain: the brain stem, the middle brain, and the neocortex. Sometimes the brain stem has been labeled the reptilian brain because it resembles the brain that developed in reptiles. The middle brain has been called the old mammalian brain since it represents the additional brain developed in the initial mammals. The neocortex represents the brain that developed in humans and other primates.

In addition, brain research identifies three functions of the brain. The first comprises the automatic functions of survival, sex, respiration, and digestion. All these occur without conscious thought. These automatic functions are centered in the brain stem.

The second function deals with emotions, memory, and social connections. Sometimes this area is identified as the limbic system. It is important to note that these functions may occur in the middle brain but that memory occurs in the neo-cortex also.

The third function of the brain is higher order thinking. Linguistic skills, analytical skills, and creative skills are all part of this third function, a lot of which is located in the neocortex.

A crucial concept in brain research is downshifting. While higher order thinking is encouraged through high-challenge tasks and situations, high-threat tasks and situations often take a person out of higher order thinking and into the emo-tional functions of the middle brain or even into the fight-or-flight, survival functions associated with the brain stem. Tasks and situations must be highly challenging but not highly threatening in order to keep people in their highest thinking level, associated with the neocortex.

Brain researchers Renate and Geoffrey Caine have sum-marized their work in the form of twelve brain principles, quoted here.

Principle 1: The brain is a complex adaptive system.

Principle 2: The brain is a social brain.

Principle 3: The search for meaning is innate.

Principle 4: The search for meaning occurs through "patterning."

Principle 5: Emotions are critical to patterning.

Principle 6: Every brain simultaneously perceives and creates parts and wholes.

Principle 7: Learning involves both focused attention and peripheral perception.

Principle 8: Learning always involves conscious and unconscious processes.

Principle 9: We have at least two ways of organizing memory.

Principle 10: Learning is developmental.

Principle 11: Complex learning is enhanced by challenge and inhibited by threat.

Principle 12: Every brain is uniquely organized. (Caine & Caine, 1997, p. 19)

Because the brain is a social brain, it is uniquely adapted to working with others. The brain can function well in association with others, provided the group uses tools and strategies that foster helpful social connections. This finding suggests that fundamentally the brain wants to connect with others. Only negative past experiences change this orientation. On the other hand, positive experiences can restore faith in connecting with others. Since the brain is geared for social interactions, leaders will do well to use well-thought-through strategies that promote interactions that facilitate consensus. "Social experience actualizes human intelligence" (Dickman & Stanford-Blair, 2002, p. 58).

The brain is constantly attempting to make sense of the data it receives. Fashioning meaning is one of its strongest functions. One way it does this is by making connections, sometimes with previously learned material, and at other times among things presently being studied. This function suggests that the more the brain is asked to make connections, the more it thrives and grows. The more the brain is called on to discern patterns, the more alive and active it becomes. This understanding makes it incumbent on leaders to provide enough information so that a team can draw helpful conclusions. This approach is far more effective than leaders' presenting their own conclusions and imperatives to a group.

Emotions play a crucial role in the functioning of the brain. A supportive and encouraging environment enhances the higher order thinking capacities of the brain. Once again, a challenging environment exercises the brain. A depressing or threatening environment only makes the brain want to get away. This fact calls on leaders to create environments that support and encourage participation and risk-taking. "Emotion is the arbiter between lower and higher brain structures" (Dickman & Stanford-Blair, 2002, p. 74).

Our new understanding suggests not only that the brain thrives on complex tasks but that it can work on many different steps of a task at once. In other words, we cheat people when we make things too easy.

A related section of brain research has focused on intelligence. Howard Gardner's extensive research has led him to propose a theory of multiple intelligences. In 1983 his book *Frames of Mind* identified seven different intelligences. In the 1990s he added an eighth. Until his theory emerged, intelligence was generally viewed as uniform, and one had either a lot of it, some, or practically none at all. Gardner proposes that everyone has a unique mixture of all eight intelligences, some of them stronger than others.

Gardner goes on to suggest that intelligences can be modified and that we can become more comfortable in our areas of weaker intelligence. People who have a chance to use and exercise their strong intelligences become more open to experimenting in their weaker ones. Imagine the implications for leadership. The adept leader finds ways to tap into many intelligences, thus bringing more and more people on board. The knowledgeable leader analyzes the strengths of colleagues and matches colleagues with tasks and assignments that capitalize on their unique sets of intelligences.

"Leadership connections to the brain have been long assumed, given the brain's mediating role in all interactions between people. Emerging knowledge about intelligence, however, presents an opportunity to tighten the brain-leadership connection—an opportunity for leaders to better understand and engage the intelligence of self and others" (Dickman & Stanford-Blair, 2002, p. 9).

If intelligence is now understood to be "multidimensional and malleable" (Dickman & Stanford-Blair, 2002, p. 19), then leadership styles and consensus approaches are called on to be multidimensional and malleable also. Leadership needs to become more alert in reading the people surrounding the leader and to amass a host of strategies to use when working with colleagues.

About Leadership

Today leadership needs to respond to a dramatic paradigm shift. The leader no longer lives in a vertical, top-down environment. There is a shift toward high degrees of participation from all levels.

> Participation, though, is not an isolated phenomenon. It is part of a wider circle of factors that define how human beings relate to one another in our times. It is a key component of the new paradigm of living in the 21st century, and as such, finds allies in other kindred disciplines such as conflict mediation, dispute partnering, and facilitative leadership, to name a few. (Troxel, 1993, p. 6)

Gone are the days when a leader could simply mandate a new direction, a new strategy, or a new product. The ideal leader taps the wisdom of every level of an organization, particularly to get the insights of those who are on the "front lines." The wise leader knows that these are the people who will carry out any new directive and who often have very practical experience to guide what will work and what will not work.

Today's leader combines many roles and wears many hats. McEwan identifies ten of these. While this list was created in the context of school principals, it can clarify the role of any leader.

1. The Communicator

2. The Educator

3. The Envisioner

4. The Facilitator

5. The Change Master

6. The Culture Builder

7. The Activator

8. The Producer

9. The Character Builder

10. The Contributor (McEwan, 2003, p. xv)

The facilitator role has become an extremely important role within the culture of participation. It is a role that guides and elicits rather than declares and demands. It is a role that is generous with information and trusting of people's capacity to make sound decisions and recommendations when the facts are known. It is a role that conveys genuine respect and appreciation for the talents and skills of colleagues. It requires enhanced interpersonal skills and genuine tact. All these requirements suggest that the facilitator role is not an easy one to play.

It is important at this point to note that a facilitative role in no way abdicates strong leadership. Rather it transforms strong leadership into a form that engenders employee buy-in and finally employee loyalty as people discover that their insights and skills are genuinely honored, appreciated, and used. The facilitative leader can experience more powerful influence than ever, and in an entirely different way. "The facilitative leader helps groups and individuals become more effective through building their capacity to reflect on and improve the way they work" (Schwarz, 2002, p. 327). Furthermore, a person can play the role of a facilitative leader even if that person is not the stated formal leader (Schwarz, 2002, p. 327). In other words, sometimes just by asking the right question at the right time, a leader can move a meeting out of a discussion getting nowhere and into a discussion leading to a decision or a solution.

As noted above, there has been a paradigm shift toward participation. One implication of this shift is that management philosophy is shifting from a top-down, one-way approach to a philosophy that encourages learning, two-way dialogue, empowerment, and loyalty (Schwarz, 2002, p. 328). Either formally or informally, management is listening to front-line workers to glean their concerns as well as their suggestions, which suggests that managers are sharing more data so that their colleagues can offer realistic proposals. Because the front-line people are empowered to make helpful decisions on behalf of the client, the potential for increasing client satisfaction grows. When people's creativity is tapped, their commitment and loyalty grow.

Supportive of this aspect of management and leadership is a principle called "distributive leadership" (Fullan, 2003, p. 24; Hargreaves & Fink, 2004, p. 10). Part of the leader's task of empowerment is to initiate colleagues into dimensions of leadership, in other words, to become a leadership trainer, imparting to others the skills and capacities the leader has developed over time and through experience. Far from diminishing the leader's role, this sharing strengthens it and, needless to say, transforms the company, organization, or institution. What may be difficult for the leader to comprehend at first is that leadership roles have become extremely complex and demanding today. The more insight, wisdom, and support the leadership dynamic gets, the more successful it will be.

Because leadership roles have become so demanding and overwhelming, leadership sustainability has become an important area of concern. "Individual sustainability concerns the ability to keep on going without burning out. The key to doing this is not an all-out marathon, but rather cyclical energizing. To do this, leaders need to seek sources and situations that push the limits of their energy and engagement, coupled with rituals or periodic breaks that are energy recovering" (Fullan, 2005, p. 35).

Fullan goes on to identify eight arenas of sustainability:

1. Public service with a moral purpose

2. Commitment to changing context at all levels

3. Lateral capacity building through networks

4. Intelligent accountability and vertical relationships (encompassing both capacity building and accountability)

5. Deep learning

6. Dual commitment to short-term and long-term results

7. Cyclical energizing

8. The long lever of leadership (Fullan, 2005, p. 14)

Note that the first element of sustainability is moral purpose. It is leaders' belief in the moral purpose of their leadership that allows them continually to renew their energy and return day in and day out to the challenges and struggles (Fullan, 2003, p. 19). Believing in their moral purpose requires continual reflection and remembering the deep reasons that at one time pushed them to enter their field of work.

Another element related to sustainability is what Fullan calls "cyclical energizing," which calls for leaders to step back, take a vacation, do something different, and so on. It requires some humility to believe that life at work will continue even with their absence. It requires trust that the work will be there awaiting their return. Those who do not find some way to reenergize themselves will lose the spark, the spirit that also helps renew colleagues. This renewed energy allows a leader to keep stretching out to the new to discern what pieces of the new will improve the organization, the company, or the institution.

Many organizations, when experiencing struggle and difficulty, bring in very high-powered, well-known, and charismatic leadership to help repair the situation. Doing this does indeed restore some energy and hope. Yet very often that energy is centered in the charismatic leader. If the leader does not enable a shared vision among many, then when the leader moves on, motivation and energy collapse. That is why charismatic leaders do not, in the end, foster sustainability in leadership (Fullan, 2005, p. 30; Hargreaves & Fink, 2004, p. 10).

Another reason is that the charismatic leader does not really understand the complex workings of the organization and therefore does not really help transform the organization's structures to help it improve.

We also have fresh insight into the crucial role of the manager. This role is different from the role of the head of an organization. The manager is closest to the front-line worker. "We had discovered that the manager—not pay, benefits, perks, or a charismatic corporate leader—was the critical player in building a strong workplace" (Buckingham & Coffman, 1999, p. 32). It is the manager who has the potential of releasing the creativity and commitment of these workers. This potential has to do with how well the manager really studies the workers and matches the tasks to the workers' strengths and abilities. In addition, if the manager is difficult to work with, rarely appreciating others' work, then workers' desire to keep working in that job fades. This potential also includes the capacity on the part of managers to trust in their workers. "They believe that if you expect the best from people, then more often than not the best is what you get" (Buckingham & Coffman, 1999, p. 117). This trust is crucial if the manager decides to rely on the wisdom of the workers. If the manager doesn't really trust the workers, the workers will not want to communicate their best wisdom to the manager. Or, "if you don't trust others, they won't trust you" (Rosberg, McGee, & Burgett, 2003, p. 104).

This discussion suggests that leadership today requires the acquisition of skills to work with colleagues. Some of these are consensus skills, some are listening skills, some are team implementation skills, and some are participation skills. In addition, the acquisition of these skills will enable a leader to become far more effective than the leader can imagine.

About Consensus

In former eras, one person made a decision and passed it down a chain of command, confident that the decision would be implemented in all the correct places. Today, people are reluctant to carry out a decision in which they have had no voice whatsoever. Furthermore, with increased confidence in their own abilities, people believe they have as much wisdom and as valid a perspective as the person at the top. Needless to say, this creates an obvious clash between leadership schooled in making top-down decisions and employees who believe their front-line wisdom is being ignored. The path out of this impasse is teamwork with consensus at its heart.

So, what is consensus? Richard Wynn and C. W. Guditus (1984) take us directly to the dictionary to define it. They remind us that *consensus* comes from the Latin word *consentire*, which means "to think together." Wynn and Guditus go on to say that the *American College Dictionary* defines *consent* as "general agreement." Based on this definition, we might say that consensus has something to do with talking and thinking together followed by some form of agreement.

It is crucial for a group to decide just what it will mean by consensus. Will it mean that everyone has to agree to the decision before it is implemented? That as long as everyone can support it, consensus has been reached? That almost everyone has to agree? That a specific percentage agrees? (Schwarz, 2002, p. 112). Groups also need to decide exactly what decisions will be made by consensus and what decisions will be made through another methodology, such as voting. Schwarz (2002) describes a consensus process that keeps everyone on board:

> Consensus decision making accomplishes [shared understandings] by ensuring that a decision is not reached until each group member can commit to the decision as his or her own. It equalizes the distribution of power in the group, because every member's concerns must be addressed and every member's consent is required to reach a decision. Making a decision by consensus can take more time than other methods, but because people are then internally committed to the decision it will usually take less time to implement effectively. (p. 133)

This statement certainly highlights the advantages of a true consensus process. By listening to all perspectives intently, the group comes up with a decision that honors as much as possible the wisdom of all in the group. Needless to say, this process will require time, but the buy-in and resulting commitment will end up hastening the implementation.

Stanfield (2002) offers a slightly different slant:

> There is considerable misunderstanding about the nature of consensus. Most people think it means that everyone agrees.

> A consensus articulates the common will of the group. Consensus is a common understanding which enables a group to move forward together. Consensus is reached when all the participants are willing to move forward together, even if they do not agree on all the details. (p. 5)

There is a great deal of tension between pushing forward until everyone is on board and can support a decision and coming to a point where just one or two people are stubbornly refusing to compromise, thus hampering the fundamental will of the group. Perhaps the best one can do in such circumstances is get agreement that the one or two who cannot or will not get on board promise not to sabotage the decision. Later on they may see the benefits of the decision. Often resistors are satisfied if their points of resistance have been clearly stated so that the group understands where they are coming from. Sometimes a question such as "Do we have enough agreement to move ahead together?" allows people to set their concerns aside temporarily and move ahead.

As another authority says, "It is possible for a group member to disagree with a particular decision but consent to support it because:

- The group made a good faith effort to address all concerns raised.
- The decision serves the group's current purpose, values, and interests.
- The decision is one that they can live with, though not their first choice." (Dressler, 2004, p. 4)

Before attempting consensus, it is crucial to determine whether a shared framework has been built with the group. Have all the facts been distributed and discussed? Have the advantages and disadvantages of various approaches and decisions been discussed? Have the insights behind these approaches been talked about? These are important steps for a group to take before it attempts consensus (Kaner, 1996, p. 149).

Consensus is both the process people go through to arrive at a mutually agreed-on decision and the product of such a process. People who participate in genuine dialogue over an issue, in the midst of real sharing of a variety of perspectives, are often willing to bend their own private opinions and desires in order to arrive at an effective group decision. That final product is a consensus. The process of thinking together, assuring everyone that each perspective is heard, and moving toward a decision is also a consensus.

When we believe that human beings are motivated solely by self-interest, then it is difficult to imagine that consensus can occur. Consensus rests on the assumption that people can voluntarily back away from some aspects of their position in order that some other aspects of their position can be satisfied in a group agreement. Robert Frank (in Mansbridge, 1990) suggests that people can care about more than just their own self-interest. Indeed, it is selling human beings short to say we are motivated only by self-interest.

In addition to whatever drive to self-interest we humans possess, there is also a drive to connect with other human beings. This potential is the foundation of the belief in the possibility of consensus. Consensus could not occur were human beings not able to think and act beyond their self-interest. The desire to connect is strong. It is the experience of feeling connected that positively motivates even those who are cynical and bitter to try one more time to work with a group of people who share issues and concerns.

About the Setting and Logistics for Team Consensus

When I am asked to work with a group, several concrete questions come to mind that may also assist you. Does the room have tables and chairs and not just a theater-style arrangement? Does the room have a working wall? Is the group number between ten and fifty? (More than fifty becomes unwieldy in terms of generating real consensus.) Can you enable as much material to be visual as possible? Other details will emerge as this book unfolds. They can help smooth your journey to consensus.

PART I

Purposeful Vision

Promoters of sustainability cultivate and re-create an environment that has the capacity to stimulate continuous improvement on a broad front.

—Hargreaves and Fink (2004, p. 12)

People want their actions and efforts to make a difference. The possibility that one's own efforts could really transform something is deeply powerful. On the other hand, cynicism and bitterness result when people sense that anything they do or think has absolutely no effect.

When we talk about consensus, we talk about reviving the hope that actions can result in something positive and affect some genuine change. The despair of our age comes from men and women who have individually been trying to make a difference for years. The issues and problems have grown so large that no one person can make much of a difference anymore. As Peters suggests, "In a time of turbulence and uncertainty, one must be able to take instant action on the front line.

But to support such action-taking at the front, everyone must have a clear understanding about what the organization is trying to achieve" (1987, p. 398). In other words, a muddled vision hampers and stifles action. Conversely, as Laura Spencer notes, a clear and concrete vision can stimulate and focus concerted action; it "provides the direction toward which an organization can move and align itself. The clearer the vision, the more focused the strategy" (1989, p. 99). Even more important is that leaders can have a lasting effect when they have gone through the effort of making sure others share and have helped to create and develop the leaders' vision (Hargreaves & Fink, 2004, p. 10).

Action that is focused and based on consensus can change many of our deep-seated issues and contradictions. People are beginning to believe that perhaps there is hope in the concerted action of a team. Clearly stating a vision and working collaboratively can create a new setting for profound consensus. "Consensus is a collaborative search for common ground solutions rather than a competitive effort to convince others to adopt a particular position. This requires that group members feel committed to a common purpose" (Dressler, 2004, p. 3). A strong awareness of purpose can do much to foster a willingness for consensus (Fullan, 2003, p. 19).

Some environments promote vision while others promote burnout. Jaffe, Scott, and Orioli (in Adams, 1986) talk about environments that promote inspired performance and vision. Environments that tap into people's hopes and dreams set the stage for powerful consensus. An environment that values individuals allows for creativity, innovation, risk taking, and honest mistakes. In such an environment, inspired minds are valued as much as productive hands.

Environments that promote vision web human beings together in teams so that human minds can be in dialogue with other human minds. One person's visions of possibility are linked with other people's visions of possibility.

An environment of vision places value on human beings and their potential for learning and creativity. Environments that are closed communicate that the answers are already known, eliminate the possibility of human innovation and creativity, and discourage any effort at authentic teamwork. The only thing that is desired in a closed environment is individual obedience and loyalty to the already-decided direction and approaches.

A well-thought-out vision invites action that can happen only with consensus. If a vision is any good, it paves the way for action. The road to action from vision passes through consensus. In other words, action cannot happen without agreement on what to do. If the process stops with articulating the vision, people soon get the idea that nothing is going to happen. On the other hand, if you create the vision and then dictate exactly how everyone is going to do his or her part, the power of that vision is soon strangled.

The process of creating a purposeful vision together often reveals the hopes and yearnings of all the teammates. People with very different perspectives and job roles suddenly begin to sense their surprising unity with others on the team. Connections are made that had seemed impossible, and the foundation for the process of consensus begins to grow.

If no time is spent on this step of building connections among people, it is unrealistic to expect serious consensus. In today's milieu of instant this and immediate that, it is difficult to convince people that the process of consensus cannot happen overnight. People need time to move from an environment of fierce competition to one of connection, cooperation, and consensus.

Current brain research has emphasized the crucial role that emotions play in the brain.

"*If* emotion is the means by which humans attend, make judgments, and are motivated, *then* the development of a common vision of meaningful purpose is important to tapping emotional commitment and passion in individuals and organizations" (Dickman & Stanford-Blair, 2002, p. 77). When individual purposes get combined into a group's purpose, energy is released toward deep commitment. Purposeful vision provides the energy for consensus and then action.

Once the leaders of an organization have fostered authentic consensus on both the vision and the action toward that vision, they can trust that the vision is now shared by all. Following this, if everyone has genuinely created strategies and actions out of that vision, then the leaders can trust more and more in the day-to-day implementation of the vision. In this way, authentic consensus permits rapid action and immediate responses.

The process of experiencing consensus is deeply energizing. If you add to this the actual accomplishment of a project, the desire to work and create more successes grows. The potential for deeper and deeper consensus builds as people experience the energizing impact of their work together.

Chapter 1

Visualizing the Common Direction: Simple Things to Do

INTRODUCTION TO COMMON DIRECTION

Direction is the end focus, the common picture of where people want to be. People expend energy toward this goal. A common direction funnels people's attention and their endeavors.

Agreement on the focus or direction is critical in setting the stage for consensus. How can there be agreement on the particular steps leading somewhere if there is no agreement on where you are going? Furthermore, the clearer the picture of the direction, the more potential there is for consensus, and the more motivation there is to reach it. Fuzzy pictures of direction only cloud the potential for consensus along the way. Once the common direction has been clearly stated and agreed on, keeping it visually before people continuously reminds them of the original agreement and thereby increases the trust level among the group members.

≈1≈

Hopes and Desires Conversation

When you begin with the end in mind, you gain a different perspective.

—Covey (1990)

Description

The Hopes and Desires Conversation is a guided conversation during which the participants state in an informal way what they hope and want for the future of their organization. If the group is small enough, everyone has a chance to say something specific about what he or she hopes for. At the conclusion, the group can name some of the common themes heard throughout.

Beneath the surface of the day-to-day grind, the nitty-gritty struggles, and the overwhelming issues lie unarticulated hopes for the future. These are crowded out very easily by the constant demands of urgent crises. When hopes and desires finally have a chance to be articulated, it is extremely easy to identify with them. Some of them are even deeply spirit filled and insightful. They raise the level of the group's thinking and feeling. A ten-minute conversation often enables connections among the participants and adds to the foundation for consensus.

Did You Know?

- Everyone hopes for something.
- Starting with hopes and desires creates energy; starting with problems and complaints saps energy.

- It is easy to forget our deep hopes when the going is rough.

Activity: Hopes and Desires Conversation

You need at least ten or fifteen minutes to do this conversation well. After everyone is seated, suggest to the whole group that you would like to take a few moments to look at the past and the future. Ask the whole group the questions below. Try to get four or five responses to each question.

1. What are some of the hallmarks of this past year or decade for our organization?

2. What are some of your own accomplishments?

3. What are some of your hopes and desires for this organization five years down the road? What do you want to see us become? What do you hope we can accomplish in five years?

4. What have you heard in these responses? What is it we all say we are hoping for?

5. For these desires to be realized, what are some of the concrete implications for us? For how we think? How we operate? How we work? How we deal with the community?

Hints

- Start with questions that focus first on the past. It has been said that people can look ahead only as far as they can look back. As you hear the answers, help the group make them as specific as possible. There is a large difference between an answer such as "hard economic times" and "the closing of the automobile plant in our town."
- Question 4 is crucial. You are helping the group see some of the commonalities in the responses. You are asking the group to connect several responses with a

common theme. People can see not only how their ideas are related but how they themselves are related. You are setting the stage for more concrete connections later on.

- Question 5 pushes the group in a very nonthreatening way to reveal some of its ideas about the actual implementation of its hopes and desires. You don't need to write anything down as you lead this discussion, but it can reveal a lot to the leader who is paying attention. Comments here may help you decide what kind of contexts to establish in future meetings. How committed people are and how the group is willing to proceed may also be revealed.

Example

Retail managers from a large department store, discussing ways to improve customer satisfaction, gave responses such as the following when asked what they hoped and desired:

- Better phone etiquette
- Department product knowledge
- More descriptive signs
- Visible aisle directions
- Weekly employee-employer meetings
- Advertised merchandise always available

After receiving fifteen or twenty responses, a leader asked, "What are some of the common themes you heard running through these responses?" The managers identified the following themes:

- On-the-job training
- Company employee recognition
- Customer direction aids
- Improved service system
- Responsive sales force

In just a short time, this group gained a sense of what it wanted to see happen.

ᔥ2ᔦ

Snapshots

Quite simply, the vision must supplant the rule book and policy manual.

—Peters (1987)

Description

When a group has already worked on its vision, then instead of having a conversation or a workshop, you can help the members summarize rapidly what they have done by encouraging small groups of two or three people to draw on chart paper an actual snapshot of some aspect of their vision, hopes, or desires. After the snapshots are collected and shown to the whole group, the group can step back and reflect on the common themes it sees in the pictures and touch bases with its vision.

It is possible to run into situations in which people are sick of doing work on vision. This state of affairs actually means that although their thinking about their vision was good, it stopped at that point. Because the group did not move beyond the vision, the members naturally became disgruntled. A snapshot or picture will seem different from what they have been doing so far.

Did You Know?

- Kenneth Boulding (1975) reminds us that images can be more crucial for change than ideas.

- Pictures can make us think more concretely than words can.
- Pictures are the basis of the entire writing system of Chinese characters.

Activity: Snapshots

1. Place some markers, chart paper, and masking tape on each table or with each working team.

2. Have each team draw on the chart paper a snapshot or picture that holds and dramatizes some aspect of its vision.

3. Suggest a time limit, such as ten minutes.

4. Have each group choose a reporter.

5. Each team's reporter will present the snapshot to the whole group and put it on the wall.

6. After all the teams have presented, ask, "What are some of the common themes running through these snapshots?"

7. Have on the wall at least ten 5×8 cards with borders drawn around them, and record the responses, one response per card.

Hints

- Assorted colors of markers for each team increase motivation.
- Repetitious pictures do not matter, and gaps in the total vision of the snapshots are OK. You are honoring the dimension of vision here; you are not after comprehensiveness at this point.
- My experience is that this activity so quickly provides a way for people to talk about their hopes and visions that their cynicism does not have a chance to show itself.

- Another advantage of this activity is that its structure ensures concreteness. If you are drawing a picture, you have to have specifics in mind. The very concreteness of the pictures provides points for real agreement and consensus among the participants.

Example

Often a facilitator is called on to work with groups who have spent months and months trying to hammer out their vision. The more the months progressed, the more discouraging and frustrating the process felt. By the time the facilitator was asked to lead a group, it was almost too late.

After giving a social agency fifteen minutes to come up with pictures, the facilitator found that the pictures revealed the following:

- Newer equipment
- Satisfied clients
- Staff working in teams around a table
- A newsletter
- More diverse clients
- Attractive marketing and public relations materials
- Staff getting new training
- Staff working and planning with the board

It was then easy to discern the following common themes:

- Effective public relations
- Accessible consumer services
- Consistent financial development
- Multidirectional communication
- Positive, proactive board development

≈3≈

Brainstorming Closure

The skill of visioning underlies each of the key elements of creating inspired performance.

—Jaffe, Scott, and Orioli
(cited in Adams, 1986)

Description

As it is helpful during a meeting for participants to see, as well as hear, the deliberations or the brainstorming, many facilitators use chart paper to record ideas brainstormed by the group. Very often, however, people do not know what to do once they have a list of ideas. The ideas just stay there and go nowhere.

Brainstorming Closure suggests that once you acquire a list through brainstorming, you enable the group to step back and discern the points of agreement in the entire list.

Did You Know?

- Many facilitators are good at brainstorming; not many are good at knowing what to do with brainstorming.
- Sometimes what people need is not more data but ways to organize and deal with the data they already have.
- Thirty pieces of information feels overwhelming to a group; seven or eight major themes seem possible to handle or respond to.

Activity: Brainstorming Closure

1. Ahead of time, prepare the questions for the group to brainstorm, such as the following:
   a. What are different ways we can market this product?
   b. Where are possible places to cut the budget?
   c. What are steps we can take to improve employee participation and loyalty?
   d. What are some simple ways we can increase customer service?

2. After individuals have had time to jot down their own responses, have teams of two, three, or four talk through some of their ideas.

3. Then ask, "What are some of the responses your teams talked about?"

4. Record on chart paper all the ideas mentioned, and attempt to get a list of fifteen to twenty ideas.

5. Next to the chart paper have eight to ten blank 5 × 8 cards in a vertical column.

6. Read the brainstormed list and ask the group what the major themes or major points of agreement are.

7. Write these points, one per card, on the cards lined up next to the chart paper.

8. Conclude by asking the group a question to help it process this information, such as:
   a. What insights have these data generated for you?
   b. What do you see as our next steps?
   c. What implications come out of this?

Hints

- If you directly open the question to the whole group, you are inviting only the quick thinkers or those with axes to grind to begin the discussion.
- If people get stuck, read over the answers to generate more responses.

- If you have time, a fuller workshop such as that described in Cardstorming (see Activity 7, in Chapter 2) is better. If all you have is twenty minutes, this is an ideal way to get lots of ideas and bring the ideas into some kind of focus.
- Note that the "points of agreement" referred to in question 6 are not individual items chosen from the brainstorm list but represent combinations of items or the idea behind several items on the list.

Example

At a recent conference, the leader asked, "What do you see going on in a school moving toward 'new vision, new action'?" (the theme of the conference). In the brainstormed list, the leader got responses such as these:

More teams

People asking questions

Clear guidelines

Restructuring teams

Staff meeting with community

Student-centered classrooms

Students working in groups together

When asked for the common themes behind the whole list, the audience often produced much more thoughtful responses:

Action groups

Student-parent-community involvement

Consensus decision making

Conflict resolving and problem solving

Empowered people

≈4≈

TV Personality in Three Years

The most powerful, driving, unifying visions share several qualities: 1. They are concrete and specific; 2. They are bold, challenging and exciting; 3. They are attainable.

—Spencer (1989)

Description

In a guided conversation, participants can be led to clearly imagine or visualize the future. Using a TV news personality and a cameraperson, you can dramatize the kind of concrete imagining you want the participants to do. Very general responses such as "people taking more responsibility" are replaced with "weekly team meetings" or "posted team reports."

By asking people to concentrate on what they can actually see several years down the road, you make their ideas more practical and concrete. This activity moves people beyond the intellectual statement of goals to a realistic image of what the goal would look like in practice.

Did You Know?

- When people imagine, they start to tap into more parts of the brain than they use in logical, step-by-step thinking.
- Seeing is believing.

- Taking people out of the present moment and down the road three years frees their imaginations from the clutter of day-to-day problems and concerns.

Activity: TV Personality in Three Years

1. Have the group choose a national or local TV news personality. Tell the group members that three years from now, this celebrity will do a special report on their organization, highlighting some successful resolutions to the concerns the group has discussed in this meeting.

2. Be sure to include the cameraperson to remind people of the necessity of the visual.

3. Suggest people put down their pens and pencils. To encourage imagining, suggest they look out the window or at the ceiling or even close their eyes. By giving them permission to imagine, you are tapping that dimension of the brain that can release some genuine creativity.

4. Each group member is to imagine hosting the newscaster and cameraperson and will therefore have to choose what to include in the video presentation.

5. You can suggest some areas or places the camera might visit: "Take our visitors first to a staff meeting. What will they see going on?" or "As our visitors walk through the offices, what will the camera capture on the walls that indicates something new is going on?"

6. When people have had a few minutes to do this kind of imagining, bring them back to the present and ask them to write down the things they have just imagined.

7. After they have had a chance to write, have them share their responses in groups of three or four for a few minutes.

8. Ask volunteers to mention the things their small groups talked about.

9. To close, you might ask, "What are some of the common themes running through our responses?"

Hints

- I encourage people to close their eyes at the beginning. I even joke that this is the only time during our work together that I will ask people to close their eyes. At the end of this imagining time, I sometimes clap my hands to symbolize that we are returning to the present.
- Do not worry if you hear some wild ideas. Remember, your ultimate goal is to discover some of the common areas of thought.
- Very often, people are astounded at how similar their visions are. You are linking people's minds and hearts together when you provide connections with what they want in the future.
- Make this a full workshop by shifting immediately to Cardstorming (Activity 7) or Brainstorming Closure (Activity 3).

Example

One facilitator I know includes the TV news personality activity as the first step of individual thinking whenever he leads the practical vision workshop in a planning session. After this, he has individuals write down the things they saw. This then provides grist for the team's sharing time.

A group concerned about home health services came up with responses like these:

- A vitalized, strategic plan
- Maximized cash flow
- Low employee turnover
- Consistent policies and procedures
- Patient satisfaction
- Community recognition
- Enhanced management skills

- Confident management team
- Kindred spirit: "We are one"

When they pulled it all together, they came up with the following common themes for clusters of responses:

- Quality patient care
- Responsive planning
- Strong, stable staff
- Cultivated growth
- Financial solvency

≈5≈

Common Direction Written Summary

Today, in some of our most successful companies, a few visionary leaders . . . have discovered a powerful tool for capturing the spirit and energy of their organizations: the vision statement.

—Richards and Engel (in Adams, 1986)

Description

Once the conversation or workshop has articulated the elements of the common direction, there still needs to be a way to tie together or relate all the major elements. A writing exercise such as this helps perform that function.

This writing exercise also allows participants to get down in writing their own understanding of the common direction. It can be done after a conversation or workshop. Each group of two or three writes its own interpretation of the common direction. Then, on hearing each team's statement, the whole group can build one common statement of the direction.

This activity provides another opportunity for creativity and genius to show forth. And indeed, when it does show forth, people are deeply appreciative of each other's thinking. When appreciation occurs naturally, more connections and ties occur that set the stage for deeper consensus as the team continues to work together.

Did You Know?

- Writing makes your workshop product available to those who were not present.
- Writing often connects the pieces of your vision into one continuous fabric.
- The process of writing helps people make the common directions their own.

Activity: Common Direction Written Summary

1. Review with the group the major elements of the common direction as discussed or worked on in a preceding workshop (e.g., "We have said that these six areas are part of our vision").

2. Reorganize the group into teams of three or four people.

3. Suggest that each team compose one paragraph to summarize and interrelate all the elements of the common direction. Give them about fifteen minutes. In addition, have them make a pictorial representation of the common direction. While they are working, they must choose a reporter to share their paragraphs and pictures.

4. After each team has completed its paragraph and pictorial representation, have each team reporter present them. Clap or show acknowledgment after each presentation. I suggest that the groups put their words and pictures on chart paper so that the whole group can see each team's work.

5. Because all the paragraphs are visible, it will be easy for the group to discern the elements and pieces that state the common direction. You can begin to build a whole-group statement of the common direction in this way.

6. When you are finished, ask the participants how their understanding of the common direction expanded or changed during this activity.

Hints

- Having all the necessary materials present is critical to the success of any activity.
- Chart paper and assorted colors of markers will encourage the teams.
- You might suggest that the teams use this simple format for their paragraphs: an introduction, a sentence about each element, and a concluding statement.

Example

In one Chicago public school, a team chosen by the local school council asked a facilitator to help the team achieve consensus on ways to relieve overcrowding at the school. After the team discerned the major events to the process of reaching consensus and put all these steps on a timeline, it decided to articulate what its bottom-line goals were. When the team members wrote the goals out, they saw that each goal could be summarized in one word. So for weeks afterward, they could say just three words (*values*, *process*, and *facility*) and remind themselves of the entire goal statement. In fact, they took the first letter of each word, V, P, and F, and created a catchy slogan: Very Positive Future.

The three goal sentences this group came up with follow. Notice that one of the three key words appears in each goal.

GOALS

I. To ensure our *values* are held in the solution.

II. To foster the growth of a *process* that involves the diverse community.

III. To develop a plan for optimizing the use of current and potential *facility:*
  A. Systems and organizational change
  B. Reconfiguring and restructuring facility and space
  C. Expand current facility or acquire more space

≈6≈

Past, Present, and Future Images

Mythos is the mechanism through which the group comes to experience its past, present and potential.

—Owen (1987)

Description

This short activity has three parts. First, the whole group brainstorms together on the past, present, and future of the organization or the team itself. After enough ideas have been generated, the group divides into three miniteams. One makes a pictorial or graphic image of the past, one of the present, and one of the future. Finally, each miniteam presents its product to the whole group. A processing question will help the members reflect on what happened during the exercise.

Daily urgent issues and concerns often crowd out the long-range perspective, making it difficult for a group to recall where it has come from and why it is meeting. This short activity will not only tap people's creativity and imagination but also remind them of the bigger picture, giving broader meaning to the tasks of the moment.

Did You Know?

- Setting the moment into the larger historical flow reminds the group that other crisis moments have been survived.
- Seeing the whole picture can put the team into a mental position to see new solutions for current issues.

Activity: Past, Present, and Future Images

1. For context, remind everyone why it is important for all of us to keep the long-range goals and the big picture in mind.

2. Have three pieces of chart paper taped on the front wall or blackboard, one labeled PAST, one labeled PRESENT, and one FUTURE.

3. Have people do some individual brainstorming to come up with phrases, ideas, or images to put in any of the three categories. Ask them to jot down their ideas or images.

4. After three minutes, ask volunteers to describe their ideas or images. List their contributions on the appropriate chart.

5. When all three pieces of chart paper have been filled, divide the group into three miniteams. Have one team work on the past, one on the present, and one on the future.

6. Give each team several minutes to come up with a picture of its assigned time period.

7. Have each miniteam share its picture with the whole group. Acknowledge each presentation in some way.

8. Ask one or two processing questions at the end, such as:
   a. "What happened to your miniteam as you worked on this?"
   b. "What insights came to you?"
   c. "What happened to your own thinking as you heard each report?"

Hints

- The mood during this activity can be very upbeat. The steps can go fairly rapidly.
- This activity could also be the first step to writing a whole story based on the ideas brainstormed under PAST, PRESENT, and FUTURE. Each team would need

to write only a paragraph on its section. Hearing this story read can be a powerful and affirming event.

Example

A division of an airline company, after brainstorming ideas and images for its past, present, and future, went on to write a brief story, consisting of a paragraph on each period. This is the written summary of the division's past, present, and future.

Higher Horizons

Remember when we were kids? And how Mom and Dad protected us? Our business and our company were much like that. The Government protected and made sure we all did the same thing. We were managed in a parent/child style. Everything was thought about and done for us. Each experience was new; exciting for you, as well as the customer. Flying was an event. Each event got bigger and faster . . . DC4, DC8, 747.

As a child, we lived in a protected neighborhood. As we entered into the '80s and adolescence, we grew in size and became a little smarter. We experimented, we began to leave the neighborhood. Kids came into our neighborhood. Sometimes, we got a bloody nose. But the real challenges were to our intellect. The old values were not so clear-cut. Technology advances were not in the size and speed of aircraft, but on systems that benefited the customer. Earning money became the most important value. Living and everyday decisions became more complex. We found ourselves on the brink of maturity.

Over a period of fifty years, we have had the opportunity to look at a rich childhood and an adolescence that stimulated intellectual growth. Our experience has prepared us for uncertain yet exciting times. We are confident that by leading and involving our people, we will all move to higher horizons.

Chapter 2

Creating Visible Documentation: Things That Take Effort

INTRODUCTION TO DOCUMENTATION

Documentation makes the results of any team meeting visible. It gets people's good thinking on paper for all to see—both right at the moment in a temporary fashion and soon after the meeting has ended in a more permanent record. While we tend to forget the details of what went on, we often remember the things we like or the things closest to our own thinking. Documentation reminds us of the whole picture.

It is the clear picture that propels us forward. The clear vision keeps us moving through each day and its often anxiety-producing details. When you have points of consensus around the vision, you can build on those consensus connections as you implement your goals. Returning from time to time to the vision (which you have permanently documented) reminds people not only that there have been many points of consensus already but that it is possible to reach consensus even on a particularly controversial issue.

≈7≈

Cardstorming

When any work team or division sees how their new project or task matters, they feel excited to call on more of their abilities and energy.

—Jaffe, Scott, and Orioli (in Adams, 1986)

Description

Many people use chart paper on a regular basis to record brainstormed ideas. During the course of any meeting, it is crucial for participants to see, as well as hear, the content of deliberations or brainstorming. It is also possible to use cards, particularly when you are delving into new ideas and want to get a sense of the clusters of data under consideration.

Most meetings become discussions among the involved or most involved personalities. Keeping the information before you on cards enables an authentic dialogue with the data. As with chart paper, it keeps the focus on the data and not on particular personalities. The advantage of recording data on 5 × 8 cards is the flexibility you have in organizing the ideas later to see the connections.

Did You Know?

- Using both verbal and spatial intelligences (as well as others) is a major step toward becoming more creative.

- Howard Gardner (1983) has identified seven major intelligences: verbal/linguistic, logical/mathematical, bodily/kinesthetic, musical/rhythmic, visual/spatial, interpersonal, and intrapersonal. In 1999 he added an eighth intelligence: naturalistic.
- Making people's thinking visible helps the group appreciate its own value.
- The discussions that occur in this activity are critical to discovering a group's consensus.

Activity: Cardstorming

1. Ahead of time, prepare the question for the group to brainstorm.

2. Give the group one very specific question at a time, explaining why it is important to deal with each question.

3. After posing the question, give people time to do their own thinking. That way, both the quick and the careful thinkers have ample time to organize their thoughts.

4. Suggest that teams of two, three, or four (depending on the size of your whole group) talk through some of their ideas. This gives people "air time" in small groups, permits some early feedback about their ideas, and relieves some of the need to use whole-group time to air their ideas.

5. Have the small teams write their ideas on the 5×8 cards, one idea per card. Ask them to use just three or four words per card. State how many cards you want each team to prepare.

6. Ask each team to pass up one or two cards. For example, you might say, "Pass up your clearest card first." Tape these on the wall at random.

7. To get a sense of the breadth of the group's thinking, ask the teams to pass up the card that is the most different from anything on the wall so far.

8. Ask the group members whether they see any connections among the cards. Cluster only the cards the group suggests are connected.

9. When clusters begin to emerge, ask the group to come up with a temporary title for each cluster. For example, if the group has clustered together cards that say "meetings more organized," "shorter meetings," and "clearer memos," it may decide to assign the title "Communication" to that cluster.

10. Label the clusters with a number, letter, or symbol.

11. Call for the remaining cards, suggesting that people write a number, letter, or symbol on cards that naturally fit into a cluster already on the wall.

12. Cards can be shifted from cluster to cluster as you get greater clarity from the additional cards coming to the front.

13. Once all the cards have been clustered, go back and clarify and polish the title of each cluster.

Hints

- Tape loops are a helpful way to attach cards to a wall. To save time, prepare some tape loops in advance.
- It is useful to get thirty to forty cards in all.
- Be sure to have the team members write in large letters on the cards.
- If you immediately open the question to the group, bypassing the small-team step, you are inviting only the quick thinkers or those with axes to grind to begin the discussion.
- I keep 3 × 5 sticky notes handy for the temporary titles for the clusters of cards.
- It is tempting to place the cards where you think they should go. Make sure you ask the group where to put each card.

- Ahead of time, think about what the group needs this information for and prepare one last question to help the group use the information it has just generated. Asking a question about the implications or the next steps gives people a chance to see the value in their thinking together. Here are examples of some possible questions: "What insights have these data generated for you?" "What are our next steps?" "What are the implications for us or for you?" "Which ideas have most appealed to you?"

Example

In working with a publishing company, a leader used cardstorming to help a group pin down the implications of its organization's five-year vision. Here are three of the group's clusters of ideas (the column headings in the table) and the corresponding images for the future.

Flexible, responsive personnel/work environment	Multimedia, multilingual products	Proactive marketing and sales focus
Larger staff	DVDs	Four-color catalog
Five project teams	Interactive video and audio training	International markets
Employee-of-the-month award	Online networking	Foreign rights legal department
Employee input into goal setting	Books in color	Marketing department
Permanent wall dividers	Publish kid books	Test marketing program

∼8∼

Meeting Products Documentation

> *To begin with the end in mind means to start with a clear understanding of your destination. It means to know where you're going so that you better understand where you are now and so that the steps you take are always in the right direction.*
>
> —Covey (1990)

Description

Each meeting needs to be planned with a specific product in mind. Getting that product down on paper, copied, and distributed, either before or at the next meeting, is a specific way of making the team's thinking visible and declaring to the team that meeting time is valuable because the product is worth documenting and printing.

Making thinking visible is a critical aspect of thinking clearly. One reason group discussion often goes on ad nauseam is that the thinking has not been documented or written down, and people repeat what has already been said. In addition, when you document the meeting products and make them available, you are creating a history of the team piece by piece. Such a clear picture of a team's past enables the team to continue to move forward with clarity and focus.

Did You Know?

- Seeing our work in print makes us feel it is worthwhile.

- Definite meeting products remind us that our time has been well spent.
- Getting our work documented helps counteract our human tendency to forget our accomplishments.

Activity: Meeting Products Documentation

Many of the activities in this book might be done before or after a meeting. This one suggests things to do both before and after the meeting.

1. Careful thought before each meeting is necessary to determine what the real product will be. If you cannot discern a product, perhaps you need to think through once more what the purpose of the meeting is.

2. If the product is a decision, then documenting the critical elements of the discussion, the possible options, or the stated values that went into the decision may be all that is needed.

3. A record of the meeting products is invaluable when it comes time to make periodic reports or if an article is needed on what has been going on.

4. This kind of printed record also can cut down on discussions or disagreements about what was decided or how something was decided.

5. Distributing this product to each person present at the meeting affirms the value of each person.

6. After you have given each person a chance to look at the product from the previous meeting, you might ask:
   a. What do you notice now, after seeing this in print?
   b. What are some of the messages this product communicates?
   c. What changes would you make to improve this?

Hints

- Having the chart paper or cards on which you wrote down the group's ideas will be helpful when you create the meeting product to print and hand out at the next meeting.

- Such documentation will help people who were absent and enable their fuller participation at the next meeting.
- If you were not able to finish the product in one meeting, either print exactly how far you got or keep the chart paper you used, bring it to the next meeting, and finish it.
- If you have difficulty leading the meeting and writing things down at the same time, have one of the team members do the writing job while the meeting is going on. That person can both participate and write things down for everyone to see.
- For meetings that last a couple of days, you may want to have someone right there typing things up as the activity progresses. Rather than annoying the participants, this arrangement adds a fine sense of drama, especially if people sense they are going to get the documentation, perhaps even before the session concludes.

Example

For seven months, a facilitator worked once a week with a team to create a community consensus on an issue facing a school. At least one clear product resulted from each of the meetings. These products were each typed, copied, and distributed at the following meeting. Here is a list of some of these products:

- Six-month plan
- Narration or description of the phases of implementing the plan
- List of subteam members
- The team's brainstorming about elements of an effective team, a team that works
- Meeting flow of a workshop the team was planning
- Values the team wanted its results to embody
- Three broad goals for the team
- List of solution options
- Three broad solution scenarios

❧9❧

Artifacts

The sense of personal power, the belief that one can make a difference, is one of the key elements in inspired performance, and in determining personal health.

—Jaffe, Scott, and Orioli (in Adams, 1986)

Description

Traditionally, verbal reports are used to give information about how things are going. Another way to give information is to bring concrete objects that represent some aspect of the things that are going on. Objects associated with a team's projects and accomplishments in the past help make what you are saying very real. If you are leading several teams, you might even suggest that for the next meeting, each team bring at least one "artifact" to represent one of its accomplishments. This communicates that when the term *implementation* is used, it means that real, concrete events or products with actual results are expected from the efforts of the team.

Some people do get very clear pictures from words. Some people even get very clear pictures from a page of numbers. Other people need to see and feel concrete objects. Furthermore, it is harder for the cynics among us to deny concrete objects, whereas words and numbers can easily be fabricated or made to exaggerate what really happened. There is an "undeniability" that surrounds concrete artifacts. Artifacts become proof that the vision previously articulated has become a reality.

Did You Know?

- Sometimes we do not "get it" until we see it.
- Concrete products and artifacts help convince even the strongest doubters among us.
- Seeing someone else's use of an idea sparks a creative way we can use the same principle.

Activity: Artifacts

1. If you are meeting with a number of teams, each team can present its artifact with a brief description.

2. Following each presentation, initiate some appropriate recognition, such as applause or a word of appreciation.

3. After all the teams have made their presentation, be sure to pose one or more of these processing questions to the entire group:
   a. Which artifact do you remember?
   b. Which ones did you like particularly?
   c. What is the message communicated through all these artifacts?
   d. What are some of the things we have learned in the process of accomplishing all these?

4. This same flow could occur with just one team present, asking each person to present an artifact from his or her recent work.

Hints

- As the leader, encourage the presentations to be brief—one to two minutes. The artifact itself is the message.
- If all team members did not bring a concrete object, give them a moment to draw a picture or put something on paper to represent the project or accomplishment they wish to report on.
- The processing questions are particularly important, for they help people internalize the fact that things are

happening. There is no better way to impact the remaining doubters than with real success.

- Some people may have learned some negative lessons. "I'll never do this in this situation again, but I might do it in that one." "If I do it again, this is how I would modify it to guarantee different results." These are very valuable lessons. They acknowledge that not everything we try will work perfectly.

Example

When an organization providing home health care decided to meet to plan its second year, it was suggested the employees bring some artifacts to the meeting. Posters for their fundraising benefit, T-shirts with the name of their organization, items from a booth they staffed at a town fair, articles in the paper, tickets to benefit performances, and artwork from clients all started to fill the table. Seeing all those artifacts imbued everyone with such a tremendous sense of success that they jumped into the planning for their second year.

≈10≈

Report

People need to feel that what they are doing is meaning-ful and important and to connect that work with the over-all work of the organization, and that what the company does matters to the world in some way.

—Jaffe, Scott, and Orioli (in Adams, 1986)

Description

Preparing a report for someone outside the larger group can be very motivating. It pushes the team members to clearly articulate what they have been doing to reach the vision and the goals. A report can be an opportunity to pull together various things that have been going on and create an integrated picture of it all. Very often the team is surprised to discover all that has happened.

Reporting to someone outside the group can initiate valuable processing and reflection about what has happened so far and what the next steps need to be. It is a way to step outside the day-to-day implementation pressure and take stock of how well things are going and what kind of improvements can be made. Reporting is particularly helpful when the outside person is encouraging and insightful and knows how to offer meaningful recommendations and reflections because this kind of response reveals that the outsider has studied the report carefully and appreciates the effort that went into it.

Did You Know?

- Just knowing you are going to make a report makes you work even harder to make things happen a little better.
- Making a report is one way of being accountable for your project.
- Preparing a report assures people that their vision is becoming a reality.

Activity: Report

It has already been suggested that getting things written down and documented is one way to keep your team's vision alive and growing. Making a report is a variation on this theme. Presenting a report can be a high-energy event.

1. The key is for everyone on the team to get into the act of preparing the report.

2. A short, team workshop (using Cardstorming in Activity 7) could help pull together the structure of the report.

3. The structure can help determine how to divide the responsibility for pulling the actual report together.

4. Once again, artifacts are critical. Pictures, charts, graphs, comparisons, third-party documentation, articles, and so on all help readers quickly grasp what you have accomplished.

5. If possible, have a team member, not the team leader, present the report. This symbolizes that the accomplishments belong to the whole team.

Hints

- If your team has done a faithful job of documenting all the products from your meetings, the report will not be difficult to pull together.

- A simple, one-page report is perfectly acceptable—and may be easier to understand than a complex, twenty-page document.

Example

The time came for a school subcommittee to report to the entire local school council. It would have been possible to give the council just the particular recommendations the subcommittee had come up with. However, the subcommittee members became very involved in making this report. They had pulled together a history leading up to this issue, some critical factual data, a record of their planning and training processes, all the data gathered from the various stakeholders during focus group sessions, and the analysis on which the subcommittee had based its recommendations. The subcommittee compiled an amazingly complete report and then used the report opportunity to get the council to discuss the subcommittee's next steps. The entire twenty-five minutes became an upbeat event rather than a boring report.

⇌ 11 ⇌

Wall Decor of Meeting Products

Effective visions are lived in details, not broad strokes.

—Peters (1987)

Description

The decision-making process is greatly enabled when relevant meeting products are kept on the wall so that meeting participants can constantly refer to them. These products may be no more than three or four sheets of chart paper with the relevant discussion points of the last meeting written on them.

Keeping meeting products on the wall forces team members to focus on the issues at hand. It keeps their thinking on track as the group moves toward consensus, and it keeps the actualization of the vision continuously in view.

It is important to communicate to individuals that their ideas are important. Team members look on the wall and see that an idea they mentioned last week is still there. People do not have to keep proving themselves because their contributions are visible and continually referred to as meetings progress. When team members walk into the room and see the products posted on the wall, suddenly the space becomes theirs (even if it is not always theirs).

Did You Know?

- Being surrounded by the products of hard work can provide the kind of energy stained glass windows provide people who enter Gothic cathedrals.
- Posted meeting products remind us that our team is winning.
- Seeing our past meeting products helps us focus on where we are headed in the future.

Activity: Wall Decor of Meeting Products

This activity involves your time before and after the meeting, and it concerns your meeting space. With this activity, you are setting the stage for the drama of your meeting.

1. As you think through the products needed at the next meeting, think back on past discussion material and meeting products to determine which will be the most useful for the next meeting.

2. Arriving a few minutes before the meeting can give you time to put those pieces of paper on the wall before people get there. In doing this, you are claiming that space for your team, even if only for the hour you are meeting together.

3. More than likely the space is also used by others, so it will be necessary to remove everything between meetings.

Hints

- I suggest that even after you type up a product from a previous meeting, keep the chart paper or cards to post on the wall at the next meeting. Gradually, as material becomes irrelevant to current discussions or a future meeting, it can be removed.

- You might store meeting products for a while; you never know whether something will be needed for an unexpected discussion three or four weeks down the road.
- Remove the masking tape each time you take the paper down to avoid the tape sticking several of your sheets together and thereby damaging them.
- The extra time you spend putting up and taking down these meeting products may reduce the time you have to spend explaining something already discussed at length.

Example

A facilitator met with one group for several months. Unfortunately, they met in a different space most weeks. She would arrive fifteen minutes ahead of time each week, not only to lay out the materials for the day's meeting but also to put up useful products of the preceding meeting.

She sensed that since the meeting space kept changing, some continuity in the wall products would be helpful, but because the focus of each meeting shifted, she chose only the previous products that had relevance to the new focus.

⪻12⪼

Article

After the vision is written, a visionary must be prepared to spend considerable time, thought, and energy helping to make it happen.

—Richards and Engel (in Adams, 1986)

Description

This activity promotes the creation of an article on some aspect of the team's work. The article will appear in a local publication or the organization's internal publication. Articles like this do not need to be very long; pictures, graphs, or charts can add to the impact.

People who sense that their work is going to be on stage tend to put extra energy and focus into the task. A lot of us get additional excitement about our work if we know that people outside are going to learn about it. By translating the hard work of a team into an article, you are helping "tell the story," which helps sustain the purposeful vision as it continues to unfold.

Did You Know?

- Writing an article declares some good news to those around us.
- Sharing our work in an article may help change someone else's mood for the better.
- Writing an article creates pride in the whole team.

Activity: Article

1. Have the team decide how often an article needs to appear in a local or internal publication.

2. Brainstorming possible articles or article content can help use the whole team's wisdom.

3. Encourage any gifted writers on the team to send articles to a local publication.

4. Writing an article can also be assigned to pairs of people on the team.

5. Or the team may decide to set aside a little time before each article is due and create the article as a whole team.

6. Be sure to display the published articles and make mention of them.

Hints

- Simplicity that leads to regularity is more important than one massive effort that never occurs again.
- Deciding on the particular focus of each article as a team each time may make it easier to remember why the whole writing effort is important.
- A similar impact on the team can occur if one of the team accomplishments makes it to a news spot on TV. This kind of attention and recognition can go a long way in sustaining the work level and motivation of the team.

Example

Seven months after a planning and implementation session that created Partnership Projects to foster business-education partnerships in a community, an article appeared in the local Sunday paper that summarized what had happened so far.

The article emphasized that students would have a lot more contact with businesspeople during the coming school year because business and industry leaders had begun to see that contact with students in schools could have a positive effect on the work force they would be hiring in a few years.

One practical way in which the partnership implemented this contact was by inviting a principal, a teacher, and a student to join a businessperson for lunch. The intent of the lunch would be to begin a dialogue between schools and businesses.

Other initiatives would bring business and industry representatives into the classroom to talk directly about opportunities and needs for jobs in the future.

The planning team had come up with a great idea and let the whole community know about it through the article, increasing support and commitment for the partnership effort in the entire community.

Chapter 3

Illuminating the Total Framework: For the Committed

INTRODUCTION TO THE FRAMEWORK

People hunger to see the whole picture; they are lost without some sense of the total framework. Too often when we delegate only slices of the whole pie, the old framework falls apart and no longer makes sense. People need to build a new framework that puts the purpose-filled vision in a broader context. Purposeful vision provides the why of daily actions and offers the full story behind that vision. People who are enabled to see the total framework can become more willing participants in the implementation of the vision.

Consensus on the total framework is a foundational step to creating consensus on various action strategies. In fact, consensus on the total framework can release creativity in the mapping of implementation strategies. Illuminating the total framework opens people's consciousness to a new level, releasing unexpected energy toward the desired outcomes. In this way, the total framework begins to tap the profound commitment so crucial to a group's authentic consensus.

⇒13⇐

Journey Wall

Effective visions prepare for the future, but honor the past.

—Peters (1987)

Description

This is an extremely powerful activity for a group that has been around for a while. It enables new members to get on top of the history and background of the group very quickly. It also provides a tool for awakening the original vision and hopes that the long-time members brought to the inception of the group. In addition, this activity reminds the group of the historical and community events that provided the context for the group's beginning.

Through this brainstorming of events in the world, the community, and the organization or group, people begin to see the kind of connections that foster the motivation of the group.

Did You Know?

- The big picture of the way your company or organization grew out of happenings in the world around it can provide new appreciation for the role it plays.
- This activity can be the beginning of a powerful story about your company or organization.

- Seeing the chunks or phases of the organization's growth can assist the group in imagining the next phase.

Activity: Journey Wall

1. Determine the years the group or organization has been around.

2. Across the top of a blank wall in front of the group, list the years it has been in existence. Use five- or ten-year increments if necessary to make the time frame manageable.

   Examples:
   1997 1998 1999 2000 2001 2002 2003 2004 2005 2006
   or
   1965 1970 1975 1980 1985 1990 1995 2000 2005

3. On the same blank wall, down the left side, list these three major categories: World Events, Community or Local Events, and Group or Organization Events.

4. Have individuals silently brainstorm events in all three categories since the group's inception. Give them three minutes for each category.

5. Have individuals write two or three significant events in each category on 5×8 cards.

6. Then have them put the 5×8 cards on the wall, watching to make sure they place the cards in the correct row and in the approximate year column.

7. When this is finished, the wall should be covered with a large number of cards in each of the categories and across the entire span of years.

8. The purpose of the following series of questions is to help the group (1) start absorbing the mass of information on

the wall and (2) begin to discern the "chapters" of the story they are creating on the journey wall.

   a. In the World Events row, which cards stand out to you?

   b. What relationships do you see among the World Events cards?

   c. In the Community or Local Events row, which cards do you notice especially? What connections do you see among the events or happenings there?

   d. In the Group or Organization Events row, which cards were you glad to see up there? Which of these cards seem to flow together?

   e. Across all the cards, where do you see connections among the world, community, and organization events?

   f. Where would you make three or four major breaks in this organization's history?

   g. What title would you give to each of the three or four sections of this organization's history?

   h. How would you complete this title for the whole history: "The Great Story of _____"?

9. You might try a processing question to end this activity, such as: What happened to your understanding of this organization as you participated in this Journey Wall?

Hints

- You can have different topics down the side. When working with a group of educators, for instance, you could substitute Events in the World of Education for Community or Local Events.
- You can use Events in the World of Education as the first row, Events in My Own Life for the second row, and then Group or Organization Events for the third row. The nature of the group and your task will provide clues to the categories to use.
- You can do additional things with this Journey Wall. You can ask people what kind of music they hear in

each of the sections. You can ask people what colors or
sounds go in each section. One group created a pan-
tomime dance for each section of the story!

Example

The Great Story of Responding to a People's Needs				
	Feeling our way	Growing in confidence		Expanding our service
	1986–1990	1991–1995	1996–2000	2001–2005
World events	Corazon Aquino elected in Philippines Berlin Wall collapses Collapse of Soviet Union Tiananmen Square *Challenger* disaster	Election of Clinton-Gore Gulf War Rise of personal computers Somalia challenge Mandela elected in South Africa Proliferation of cell phones	Rise of the Internet Death of Princess Diana Hong Kong reverts to China John Paul II visits Cuba Panama Canal reverts to Panama	September 11 War in Iraq Terrorist attacks in Bali, Madrid, London Tsunami in Southeast Asia Hurricanes in the United States
Local events	Citywide needs survey Tornado disaster	Major industry moves to Texas New City Cultural Center Influx of Asian refugees	New statewide industry campaign Flood damage New tax system	Current mayor elected Downtown fire New industry relocates to area
Organization events	Organization formed 10 employees	4 more locations Print newsletter 2 additional departments	National recognition Major fundraising campaigns First statewide conference	100 employees Total computerization International liaisons

≈14≈

Global Events Conversation

Effective visions make sense in the marketplace, and, by stressing flexibility and execution, stand the test of time in a turbulent world.

—Peters (1987)

Description

You may not always have the amount of time necessary for the luxury of a Journey Wall. In that case, in ten to fifteen minutes you can still have a great impact with a global events conversation. This series of questions produces enough data and participation to help people see that whatever they are dealing with in their organization or community is related to things that are happening all over the world. Furthermore, at the very end, when the question of positive trends is asked, people can discern that powerful historical and global forces can be harnessed on behalf of their future.

Did You Know?

- Feeling connected to the whole world empowers people.
- Expanding your sense of belonging deepens your sense of responsibility.
- Linking yourself to the world alters your consciousness.

Activity: Global Events Conversation

Below is the series of questions you can use with a whole group. Look for several responses to each question. Do not worry about a few seconds of silence as people collect their thoughts after you ask a question.

1. If you are dealing with a specific organization, you can phrase the questions to focus on the organization's area of interest; for example, "What has been going on around the world and around the nation that has impacted the education community (or the health community or the world of finance)?"

2. Similarly, what has been going on around the state or region that has impacted your organization?

3. How have you experienced this? In other words, what are the concrete impacts of these events on your situation?

4. What creative and positive responses to some of these issues have you read about, heard about, seen, or tried yourself?

5. As we do our planning today, what are some of the broad, positive trends you want to capitalize on in some way?

Hints

- If participation seems to be a problem or if only one or two people are participating, you may want to ask for everyone to respond to some of your questions.
- Remember that you are not looking for a total, comprehensive list of responses. You want concrete answers so that once there is a general sense of the answer, you can move on to the next question.
- With a very alert group, I have added a final question to encourage their thinking about the reasons behind

using this conversation: "Why have I started our workshop session today with this conversation?"

- The tricky thing about leading this kind of conversation is that it is not a time for speeches. You want a mosaic of responses. Consequently, when you begin to get long answers, repeat the question, adding a little direction such as "in a phrase" or "by just mentioning the event." In addition, this conversation is not the time for debate or disagreements. In a sense you are building a verbal montage and then stepping back and talking about it. This conversation can happen very powerfully in just fifteen minutes.

- You might note whether there are obvious gaps in the responses. If people have given responses only about the world and haven't mentioned anything nationally or vice versa, you can prompt people to think of some events from the neglected area. Remember that your role is to lead. It is not necessary for you to contribute any responses at all.

Example

A health care organization needed to get some perspective on issues it was struggling with. The following global events conversation helped set the tone for the day.

I asked, "What has been going on around the world and nation that is affecting your business?" The group responded with the following list:

- Outsourcing
- Competition from other countries
- High cost of health care
- Rising cost of oil
- Technological advances
- Environmental consciousness

My next question was, "What has been going on in the state or local region that is affecting your business?" The answers were as follows:

- Rise in local taxes
- Companies have moved to other regions
- State regulations
- Company locations have shut down
- Small businesses struggling with high health care costs
- Diversity in the workplace

Then I asked, "How have you experienced this?" and got the following answers:

- Hard to find qualified employees
- Downsizing
- Low employee morale
- Employees must pay for part of their health insurance

When I asked, "What creative and positive solutions are you observing?" members offered the following:

- Employees participating in appropriate management decisions
- Emphasis on employee retraining
- Streamlining of previously complex procedures
- Employee recognition programs

My last question was, "What are some of the broad positive trends we want to capitalize on?" The group had the following answers:

- Rapid technological advances
- Increase in team-shared decision making
- Increasing global mobility
- Lowering of traditional East-West boundaries
- Rise in alternative medical approaches

☙15☙

Newsletter

The origin of the vision is much less important than the process whereby it comes to be shared. It is not truly a "shared vision" until it connects with the personal visions of people throughout the organization.

—Senge (1990)

Description

Depending on the nature of the team, regular communication with an appropriate constituency might be helpful. Even something fairly simple could have a big impact. One sheet of paper every month, summarizing some key happenings, could go a long way. Making it imaginative and having it focus on just two or three things could do a lot to communicate what your team has done. This step is particularly useful when little communication is going on and there is a felt need for more.

Getting the word out about what you are doing increases motivation and commitment toward your work. A newsletter can also be a vehicle for sustaining the vision that brought a team or group together in the first place. The feedback generated from such communication is also extremely valuable.

Did You Know?

- A newsletter can signal "Wake up! Something is happening!"

- A newsletter keeps reminding people of the power in their own thinking and doing.
- Seeing things in print makes the items, the events, or the issues feel more real.

Activity: Newsletter

Because a newsletter reminds a team that its vision is becoming a reality and that its efforts are making a difference, this activity cements the team and adds to its sense of connection, a critical component of consensus.

1. If such a regular communication vehicle as a newsletter does not fit your particular situation, perhaps Activity 12, Article, will fit better.

2. Meeting Products Documentation (Activity 8) is critical to providing regular documentation, some of which may be very appropriate for use in a newsletter.

3. If providing such a newsletter is a genuine team decision, then its implementation can also be a team effort. It is not meant to place another burdensome task on the back of one person or the leader.

4. A ten-minute brainstorm every so often can give enough grist for the content of each edition. Do this brainstorm on chart paper so that you can save it.

5. Check in regularly with the team to see if the timing of the newsletter is still appropriate. If once a month seems too burdensome, how about once every six weeks? If the team is excited and if lots of helpful feedback is coming as a result of the newsletter, maybe once every two or three weeks is better than once a month.

Hints

- These days many desktop publishing programs and tools with newsletter templates are available for either

PCs or Apple Macintoshes. If your team decides a newsletter fits your situation, my general guideline for getting started is simplicity.

- One page done extremely well is better than four pages done poorly.
- The external function of this newsletter is getting the word out. The internal function can be just as critical: telling the story and keeping the vision alive and expanding.

Example

A group planning and implementing business and education partnerships in a town in Wisconsin initiated a joint effort called Partnership Projects. The group also initiated a very simple newsletter called *Partnership Projects UPDATE*. One issue featured articles with the following titles:

September (a review of what was to happen that month)

Invention Convention (a report on one of the projects developed at the original planning workshop)

Job Shadowing (a report on another project that grew out of the original planning workshop)

Our School District Adopts Business/School Partnership

Logo Development (a report of the development of a Partnership Project logo, to be used on all further written communications)

⤖16⤕

Organization Principles Workshop

People need "guiding stars" to navigate and make decisions day to day. But core values are only helpful if they can be translated into concrete behaviors.

—Senge (1990)

Description

When a group has just recently come together or when you have a group that is very divided on a concern, discerning the total framework of principles can create a powerful ground of agreement and can enable real consensus.

When people put aside their anxieties about particular emotional concerns, they become surprised at the tremendous agreement they have on what they really want. By turning their attention to the valued principles they wish their solutions to embody, they begin to see that perhaps the factions within the group have important principles in common after all and that those principles form a basis for trust, negotiation, and compromise.

Did You Know?

- Valued principles touch people more deeply than money.
- Valued principles give meaning to people's work.
- Consensus on principles taps a deep commitment in people.

Activity: Organization Principles Workshop

1. Give a short introduction, explaining why you are suggesting the group spend some time looking at its valued principles.

2. Have the group members do some individual thinking for a few moments about what principles they want their organization to represent.

3. In groups of two or three, have them talk through what they feel are some of the most important principles.

4. Have them choose the five or six most critical ones and write them on 5 × 8 cards.

5. Once each miniteam has completed its cards, gradually call for the cards to be turned in. For example, have the groups pass up their clearest one first. See Activity 7, entitled Cardstorming.

6. As you tape the cards on a wall, ask the group which cards should be clustered together.

7. When all the cards have been passed forward and several clusters have been created, have the group title each cluster.

8. The result represents the whole framework of your group's valued principles.

9. Ask one or two processing questions about the valued principles: "What surprises or pleases you about this picture of our principles?" "What does this reveal to us?"

Hints

- Keep people focused on the subject of principles and not on their concerns for solutions.
- Although a group does not need to like every card on the wall, it is realistic to hope that the titles of the several clusters are principles the whole group is

behind. This may give the group its first sense of authentic consensus.

- At this point you may be able to move the group to questions such as "What does this say about what we want our organization to look like concretely?" or "What specific directions or programs would hold these principles?" Or you may be able to proceed to a question of actions: "What concrete actions could bring about an organization with these principles?"
- Depending on the mood of the group, you might even be able to ask, "What happened to us as a group as we went through this workshop?" Again, you hope that people are starting to experience some genuine connection with each other or a sense of working as a team.

Example

When a leader began a six-month process with a group, he asked this question: "What presuppositions, values, guidelines, and hopes do we have for this process of creating a solution that is based on consensus?"

The group members decided these were some of the values the process would embody:

dynamic, open-minded process

obstacles are opportunities

collaborative teamwork

climate of respect

definite and positive results

❧17❧

Purposeful Vision Chart

A vision statement is a document around which an orga-
nization can build its culture, as American culture is
built around the Declaration of Independence and the Bill
of Rights.

—Richards and Engel (in Adams, 1986)

Description

This activity creates a simple chart by means of the
Cardstorming technique described in Activity 7. This full
workshop draws individual hopes for the future of the organization into a total picture of what the group desires.

This picture is really the starting point for any serious
planning or goal setting a group needs to do.

Did You Know?

- People take personal ownership in a product that represents their own thinking and effort.
- Presenting a group's vision in an organized chart can
  make the vision appear more realizable.
- Returning to such a chart a few months later helps identify the areas that are already active as well as the areas
  that need more attention.

Activity: Purposeful Vision Chart

1. After explaining why the group is working on vision at this time, ask the group members what concrete things they see happening in their organization a few years from now.

2. Give people individual time to jot down some answers.

3. Have people talk through their ideas in teams of two or three.

4. Then have the teams write several responses on 5 × 8 cards in large letters, keeping their total words to three or four per card.

5. Ask each group to pass up one of their cards, perhaps the clearest one.

6. Attach these cards to a front wall using masking tape loops.

7. Ask for more cards, perhaps the most different card from each team.

8. As you attach these to the front wall, ask the group to note possible relationships among cards.

9. Move those cards together so that gradually clusters are formed.

10. After attaching some temporary titles to the clusters, assign a number, letter, or symbol to each cluster.

11. Ask the groups to assign the appropriate number, letter, or symbol to their remaining cards if those cards naturally gravitate toward one of the clusters.

12. Ask for the rest of the cards.

13. Talk through the cards not yet clustered to see where they belong.

14. After placing all the cards in clusters, proceed to polish the temporary titles of the clusters into specific statements of what each cluster represents in the vision of the group.

15. As a processing question, I often ask individuals to name which cluster particularly interests or excites them.

16. Be sure that someone types this product into a chart that will be available for the next meeting.

Hints

- Read Activity 7 on Cardstorming first.
- With any group, when you are working on planning, always begin with where you want to go, not with the problems or obstacles you are already facing. Beginning with problems or obstacles sets a negative tone for your work right from the start.
- After getting a noun that identifies a cluster, ask the group for two or three adjectives to clarify precisely what is represented by that cluster.
- Be sure to allow up to an hour to accomplish this activity.

Example

A group from a bank concerned about improving customer service used this activity to develop the following chart representing its three-year purposeful vision.

NORTHTOWN NATIONAL BANK The 3-Year Practical Vision				
Improved customer services		Profitable growth and expansion	Expanded training and equipment	
Customer convenience services	Customer- oriented organizational efficiency	Broader market base Cross- training	Individualized customer service training	Advanced time-saving equipment
More advanced teller terminals Call in your check order on voice mail Expand ATM locations Online banking	Bulk filing to save time Less turnover of staff Quicker loan processing Customer input Capitalize on long-term local experience	Expand to one more facility Concierge in lobby Broader advertising	Courteous, prompt, efficient service Better equipped to service more sophisticated clients Have salaries increased Better communication with other departments	More computers and PCs More-modern phone system Statements online

≈18≈

All the Stakeholders

One way for leaders to leave a lasting legacy is to ensure that others share and help develop their vision.

—Hargreaves and Fink (2004)

Description

This activity builds awareness of the value of involving representatives of all the affected stakeholders in creating solutions. This activity helps people in charge relax their initial desire to involve just a few people to maintain control of the outcomes.

Did You Know?

- Over the years, businesses have discovered the value of having people closest to the front lines participate in resolving critical issues and concerns. Being closest to the issue, these people are often most aware of the winning ways of solving an issue.
- The gift of consensus is found in the diversity of perspectives represented. The consensus is more powerful when it comes out of all these perspectives.

Activity: All the Stakeholders

1. Brainstorm all the categories of constituents affected by an issue.

2. Create a matrix with two rows, one labeled Constituents and one labeled Benefits.

3. Across the constituents row, write the various constituents brainstormed in step one.

4. Then name the benefit or benefits that could result from involving them.

5. Name any concerns that might arise from involving any of these constituents.

6. Suggest actions that might address these concerns.

7. Have the group members reflect on how their thinking has changed during this activity.

Hints

- If people are stuck coming up with a benefit, a simple sentence with a blank at the end could help, such as "Involving the support staff would be a good idea because _____."
- Sometimes a negative version of the statement could be helpful: "Leaving out the support staff would not be wise because _____."

Example

A school district decided to begin a strategic planning and implementation process. Initially it suggested having just the principals, assistant principals, and some district administrative staff attend. The facilitator suggested including some teachers, parents, community members, and even students. While it seemed strange to the planners at first, they thought through the potential benefits of having these constituencies participate, and then they went ahead and involved all the constituencies. In the end each constituency was impressed by the seriousness with which the other constituencies took the opportunity to participate. It seemed they were most grateful for the enthusiastic and perceptive participation of the student representatives.

PART II

Participative Processes

When people are invited to come together to share their ideas, concerns, and needs they become engaged. They move from being passive recipients of instructions to committed champions of decisions. This is the power of deciding together.

—Dressler (2004)

A new sense of work values the participation of every individual in the creation of organizational directions. There is a growing sense that its human resources are perhaps the most valuable asset an organization has. In addition, organizations are discovering that not only a person's hands but also a person's head and commitment can enhance total effectiveness. More succinctly, ignoring an individual's passion and concern is ignoring a huge resource. Only with participation and consensus can that passion be tapped for the sake of the work of the organization.

What are called for are ways to tap the wisdom and creativity of the entire staff or workforce. The issues are too huge and complex to permit responses and solutions to come from only a handful when the entire staff has huge mental resources and energy that can be tapped. Benefiting from that vast pool of wisdom and creativity calls for letting people know the crucial data necessary for informed decisions. Releasing those data means trusting people with information until now often reserved for just a few.

Another way to use people's wisdom and motivation is to create connections between individual aims and whole-organization goals. In other words, the process of genuine consensus starts from individual desires and hopes and moves to building whole-organization strategies and directions. When this process is done well, it taps deep personal energy for carrying out the work of the organization. A brainstormed list of ideas is a fine first step. But moving beyond the list to sensing what the list means is absolutely crucial.

In other words, participation alone is not enough. People want to see that their participation is going somewhere and is making a difference. People want to see a connection between their ideas and what actually occurs in the life of the organization. The only way to move from mere participation to committed action is through genuine consensus. Participation leads to ownership only when there has been consensus; that is, when there has been a sense of the individual pieces coming together to form some kind of organized whole.

Spencer (1989) suggests that underneath the despair and cynicism that many people are manifesting today is a deep desire to pour their energies into something that will work. While people want to make this kind of commitment, they want to participate in what they will be committed to. If they desire to be committed to something larger than themselves, they want to see some piece of themselves in that larger thing.

Genuine participation itself is complex. It is part of a whole, growing, and directed process. Participation is part of the big picture of directing and leading an organization. Participation is not something you do just once, and it is not something that can be turned on at the whim of some leader or group of leaders. Participation is an ongoing mode of operating, and organizations require new sets of skills in order to initiate and sustain genuine participation on the part of their people.

Now add to this the fact that today, beyond the dynamic of participation, there is further complexity. The staff of any organization is more diverse than ever before. Often it is multiracial, multiethnic, multireligious, and multiage. Furthermore, many problematic issues are often located not just within the organization itself but may be endemic in the entire society. All this is to say that creating consensus in the midst of this kind of complexity and diversity may be more difficult than ever before in our society.

Although these obstacles may look overwhelming and impossible to resolve, they also point us in the direction of the solution. The diversity we meet in the workplace is precisely the key to solutions. With appropriate skills, we can use that diversity to create solutions that are born of consensus. The wealth in perspective and creativity can assist in solving the concerns and issues we face.

Managers, leaders, and principals who attempt to keep their hands in everything will soon discover it is totally impossible to do so. They can head only toward burnout or more participative, consensus-generating modes. The reason is simple: No one person can be expected to have all the answers today. The issues we face are overwhelmingly complex. The world, contemporary technology, and our ever-changing society have become so complex that only a multitude of minds and perspectives can possibly succeed in uncovering workable solutions.

Four core values of participation are full participation, mutual understanding, inclusive solutions, and shared responsibility (Kaner, 1996, p. 24). Full participation suggests that the methods used invite everyone to contribute and say whatever they are thinking. When participation is skillfully encouraged, people are willing to share even ideas that aren't completely fleshed out. Mutual understanding means that everyone in the group works hard to understand the perspectives and values represented in others' ideas. Often an idea that seems contradictory to the direction the group has been moving toward will make a great deal of sense when the underlying values are explored and discovered. Inclusive solutions mean that solutions obtained by pulling together all the perspectives and needs of a group often turn out to be much better than a solution based on just one person's or segment's perspectives and needs. Drawing out the people who may find it difficult to speak up calls for skill. Shared responsibility suggests that when all the above have happened well, there is a natural desire to commit to the implementation and the consequences of the decisions made.

There are huge benefits to authentic participation. "The benefits of participation—improved relationships, altered assumptions and beliefs, shared goals and purposes, increased maturity and cognitive complexity—emerge in a spiraling way: the greater the participation, the greater the development; the greater the development, the higher the quality of participation" (Lambert, 2003, p. 12). Lambert is suggesting that as the successes of participation grow, so the desire to participate will grow stronger and deeper.

A big concern is that methods not be "coercive or manipulative."

> Finally, consensus is not a coercive or manipulative tactic to get members to conform to some pre-ordained decision. The goal of consensus is not to appear participative. It is to be participative. When members submit to pressures of authority without really agreeing with a decision, this is known as "false consensus," which ultimately leads to resentment, cynicism and inaction. (Dressler, 2004, p. 3)

False consensus will finally undermine the efforts of a group. This is why leaders think through carefully which decisions really need consensus and which decisions can be arrived at by other means. Consensus may take more time, but consensus will result in far more effectiveness.

"Even the desire to participate or to have participation is not enough. Participation involves team members acquiring a new set of skills" (Blake, Mouton, & Allen, 1987, p. 127). Because of the increasing complexity, consensus requires learning new skills appropriate to the more participative and facilitative environment of today's workplace.

Gradually, as these skills are used, people will become more and more comfortable and confident with them. The very use of these skills often pits those attempting to use them against a consciously or unconsciously hostile environment. Many times a facilitator has been asked to facilitate participative planning, only to discover that the leader who asked had no actual desire to empower the staff or employees at all. It is as if the leader only wanted to facilitate the continuation of top-down leadership.

Consensus refers to lateral connections. Powerful lateral connections are rightfully a threat to strong top-down hierarchies, a fact that adds even more dimensions to the complexity of genuine consensus. In addition, powerful lateral connections are precisely what enhance the possibility of consensus.

Chapter 4

Generating Total Participation: Simple Things to Do

Introduction to Participation

Genuine participation is difficult to achieve. It is easy to criticize early efforts to create authentic participation. It is also easy to note the faults in some of the early products. Trusting that full participation is absolutely vital to whatever goal a leader might have does not come naturally. It is easy, on the other hand, to fall back on tried-and-true top-down approaches. Sometimes this happens very subtly. Many well-intentioned leaders begin, "Now I want everyone to participate in reaching this decision." Then these same leaders proceed to talk nonstop for thirty minutes. Participation is blocked from the start. Other leaders allow a few comments, but soon they jump in, sensing a need to defend a position, comment, or action.

Many times, leadership just does not have the tools to release genuine participation. More often than not, people either fear such participation or do not really trust that full participation can achieve powerful results.

On the other hand, people are in no mood to consider consensus if they feel their voice is never heard. The truth is that some people are willing to move toward consensus and trust the group just knowing the group has heard their point of view—even if the final position has modified and altered their suggestion. Unguided participation does not in itself breed trust or automatically move a group toward consensus. Furthermore, people's relationship to participation sours if some tangible result is not evident. People will depart from the old, authoritarian ways only if some care is given to the focus and direction of participation.

People yearn to feel that their insights are welcomed and even trusted by their leaders. When this trust is genuine, participation is enhanced, and great human resources are properly channeled into actions and solutions.

∞19∞

Creating the Real Question

Participation in decision-making offers employees valued opportunities to align personal goals with those of their companies and enhances the meaningful nature of their work.

—Spencer (1989)

Description

In this activity, people write down the question they think it is critical for the particular meeting to address. Then the leader pulls several of these together, guiding the group in creating the *one* question the meeting will address.

This not only creates some early participation but also provides a focus for the rest of the meeting. In addition, it gives the alert leader some critical information about what is on people's minds. References to these individual questions later on in the meeting will give the group confidence that the leader has paid attention to what was said.

Did You Know?

- Helping a group figure out the real question gives the group its first experience of consensus.
- Coming up with the one question for a session provides a clean focus for the meeting.
- You can remind the group of this question if you think the meeting is getting off track.

Activity: Creating the Real Question

1. Open the meeting in an appropriate way, such as by introducing yourself.

2. Present this statement to the group: "I would like each of you to think a moment and then write down the *one* question you sense we need to address today."

3. Prepare chart paper in the front of the room.

4. After people have a chance to think and write, ask for some volunteers to share their questions.

5. Write all the questions on chart paper in the front of the room, even if some seem repetitive. If there are more than six groups, get representative questions from the groups.

6. When the questions have been shared, ask the group, "Where do you see some similarities or commonalities?"

7. Gradually work with the group to build the real question by asking, "What do you think is the one question this meeting is out to address?"

8. Indicate to the group that at the end of the meeting, the question will be checked to make sure the meeting has dealt with it.

9. Then at the end of the meeting, ask the group, "How has this meeting dealt with the real question?"

Hints

- This exercise has the potential of not only generating participation but, on a very foundational level, creating an early experience of consensus. It can generate a mood of accomplishment very early in a meeting.
- Keep the question posted up front. It will indirectly keep people focused on the top priority of that meeting.
- A variation of this activity might be used after you have created or presented a long agenda. You might ask the group to prioritize the agenda.

Example

A facilitator went to a school to lead a two-hour session on goal setting. It was not possible for him to meet with any of the staff ahead of time. About the only thing he knew beforehand was the topic, goal setting. As he saw it, there were several possible slants to this: How do I help my students set class goals? How do I help my students set their own personal goals? How do I better set goals for my own teaching?

After the introduction, he asked, "As you have thought about this session today, what is the one question you hoped to get some help on?" After jotting down their own individual responses, several people shared their questions:

How do I get goals accomplished in the class with so many interruptions?
What do I do when my goals fall apart in a couple of months?
Is it OK to readjust my goals?
How do you carry out goals when the students' academic levels are so divergent?

After writing all these responses on chart paper in the front, he moved to a blank sheet, saying, "Looking at these questions, what seem to be some common elements to them?" Gradually, the group created one question: "How can I increase my ability to get my goals accomplished for the students in the classroom?"

❧20❧

Eventful Happenings

Meetings sparked with humorous stories, celebrations of individual or corporate milestones, brief relaxation or energizing exercises or special refreshments at strategic intervals are eventful and enlivening.

—Spencer (1989)

Description

There are gifted people who can take an ordinary meeting, add pizzazz, and make an event out of it. It is easy around holidays to do something special to a meeting. It is even easier to celebrate a birthday and add something extra to a humdrum meeting. There are many things you can do to liven up a meeting, help motivate your team, and keep it going.

Eventful happenings create a mood of excitement and anticipation that relaxes people. They bond the group. They can set the stage for genuine consensus. They remind us that our colleagues in this group are great and significant human beings. When you believe that about your colleagues, you discover that you might want to come to consensus with them.

Did You Know?

- Events motivate us and call forth participation from us.
- Positive events are a way of taking care of team members.

- Eventful meetings create anticipation for the next meeting.

Activity: Eventful Happenings

This activity really suggests that you spend time every so often stepping back and thinking about where your group is and what it needs next.

1. Find ways to read the mood of your group frequently.
   a. In processing questions, ask people what the mood of the group is.
   b. Note people's expressions when they arrive and when they leave. People have arrived at my meetings after long days at work, looking completely wiped out. I watch them come back to life and become energized.
   c. Pay attention to the kinds of things that are talked about, the tone of people's voices, and the animation in their facial expressions.

2. When you see that meetings have lost their original excitement and anticipation, it is time to act by bringing something different to the meeting.

3. Is it time to:
   - Go to lunch together?
   - Celebrate a recent victory?
   - Recognize everyone in the group with something simple?
   - Sit back and recount the recent accomplishments?
   - Invite the managers in to say a few words of praise?
   - Write up what this group has been doing and get it reported somewhere?
   - See a movie together?

All these are ways to transform the ordinary into something special.

Hints

- If you are the type who does not feel very imaginative, more than likely someone with flair in your group would be delighted to liven things up a bit at the next meeting. Maybe you could name that person with a special title and rotate that title to a different person for each meeting.
- Whatever is done can communicate to people that their participation is special and valued. You can get a lot of energy and participation from people when they believe this about themselves.

Example

A group wanted to get community people and parents to attend a Saturday morning meeting to brainstorm some possible solutions to the issue of overcrowding at their school. One teacher came up with the idea of creating several short vignettes dramatizing the overcrowding issue. Twenty-five to thirty students would all have parts in these vignettes. In various scenes, these students portrayed a special education class that had to meet in the hall, seventh and eighth graders who ate lunch in the auditorium instead of the cafeteria, and first and second graders who feared to walk up flights of stairs crowded with bigger seventh- and eighth-grade students. All these minidramas clarified the issue and made it come alive. It was a dynamic event that increased attendance dramatically at this voluntary Saturday morning public meeting. Two hundred people were in the auditorium to watch the presentation, and seventy-five actually stayed for the full morning of workshops.

☙21☙

Sticker Dots

The concept of employee participation has taken hold so firmly that it is hard to find a current book about management that doesn't either promote participation or assume it.

—Spencer (1989)

Description

The Sticker Dots activity quickly reveals the mind of a group while getting everyone into the act. Members of the group place one or more dots on various items as a way for all to see where the mind of the whole group is. When all the dots have been placed, a conversation can help to process the picture the group has just created.

One important step in building consensus is helping a group see its own thinking. Sticker Dots is one way to do this. With the flurry of activity and drama, people can hardly argue with the picture that is created. It may not agree with their own thinking, but no one can question that it represents the mind of the group.

Once this picture is created, you can then begin to dialogue with the ideas represented in the picture and not with any particular personalities in the group. This focus helps people get one step away from their emotions and one step closer to consensus.

Did You Know?

- In the Sticker Dots activity, you involve everyone in creating an art form.
- This activity is great in multilingual situations.

Activity: Sticker Dots

1. Gather the materials beforehand: sticker dots (several colors if you decide to go that way; see Step 3 below), chart paper to write the various directions or ideas on, and a container or containers for the dots.

2. Ahead of time, prepare chart paper listing the various items you want the group to evaluate.

3. Decide whether people will get just one dot apiece or three colors with a different value for each color (e.g., a blue dot is worth three points, a red dot is worth two points, and a green dot is worth one point).

4. Prepare a brief introduction to the issues or the steps the group has taken to get this far. Clearly indicate the precise question or issue the dot activity is about.

5. Pass out the dots.

6. Invite all team members to come forward and place their dots onto their choices of the items listed on the chart paper.

7. Indicate that they may put one, two, or three of their dots on one choice if they feel that strongly about it.

8. Choose a couple of the following questions to help the group process what the picture is telling them:
   a. What do you notice?
   b. What surprises you?
   c. What interests you?
   d. How does this picture demonstrate the group's thinking about the issues before us?

e. What are the implications of this picture?

f. What are our next steps?

Hints

- You can use this activity at a public meeting to get a reading of even a large group's mind about something.
- If the attendance is more than sixty people, you may want to prepare two such lists and place them in different parts of the room to avoid a logjam when you call people to come place their dots.
- If you are doing this with such a large group, probably one dot per person will be adequate.
- Be sure to have a recorder tally the dots so that a report can be passed out to the group at the next meeting.

Example

The time came for a committee of a local school council in Chicago to present a variety of recommendations to the council and others attending the council meeting. The principal and committee chair each presented a short background to the issue and the process we were using to arrive at our recommendations. At that point, a facilitator stood up and reviewed the recommendations. She then gave directions for the Sticker Dot activity.

"When you come up to the list, you will find three bowls of different-colored dots. The blue dots are worth three points, red dots two points, and green dots one point. Each person can place one dot of each color anywhere on the list. You can even put more than one dot on one item."

People came forward. A lot of energy was flowing as people put their dots onto the list. It took about five minutes for forty people to place their dots. After they finished she asked, "What does the picture of dots tell us about our thinking on these recommendations?" They easily noticed where most of the dots lay and which items had received few dots. It was hard to argue about what the opinion of the group was.

≈22≈

Language

Workers also want to be treated with respect. Rather than mere order-takers, most valuable employees consider themselves to be as intelligent as their superiors and they want that intelligence to be recognized.

—Spencer (1989)

Description

Language has the potential of inviting or closing off participation. Particular words and phrases can actually enhance the atmosphere of participation. Leaders can increase participation not only by using techniques such as asking questions rather than making pronouncements (see Activity 24, Questions Not Dictums) but also by the very vocabulary and style of their language.

Language is powerful. It is also second nature to us. It is easy to be unaware of what our language does to the people around us. Especially if we are in a leadership position, we may not always get honest feedback about what we say and the impact it has.

Did You Know?

- Language can either invite and beckon or turn people away.
- Language includes both the words and the tone—either one can turn people off or call for their participation.

- Some people actually write a script ahead of time to monitor their words and tone.

Activity: Language

The Less Helpful column in the chart below includes comments that I believe cut off participation or cause people to hesitate before saying something. The More Helpful column includes alternative ways of communicating what is in the Less Helpful column.

LESS HELPFUL	MORE HELPFUL
That's a weird idea.	Could you clarify that for us? Say a little more about that.
We spent all last year resolving that.	What do you think is still unclear about that?
I don't see what that has to do with the question.	Please help me see the connection between what you've just said and our main question now.
Should we increase the support staff?	What are some things we could do to solve this issue?
Shall we cut the materials budget?	What are some steps we could take to solve this money crunch?
What do you think of my list of criteria for the new staff person?	What would be helpful qualifications to look for in our new staff person?
You've left something out.	I like your next focus on cost-cutting procedures.

Note: There are a lot of questions in the More Helpful column because well-stated questions often encourage participation better than statements do.

Hints

- If you are courageous, you might tape-record yourself at a typical meeting. When you play the recording back, listen for things you said that seemed to occasion responses. Then pay attention to things you said that brought a lot of silence. Try to figure out what made the difference. It may have just happened that way—or it may have had something to do with what you said or how you said it. Note the tone of your voice. Does it invite participation?
- If you have been in a leadership position for a long time, much of what you do and say is by now very natural. You might try writing a script for yourself for your next meeting. Write down exactly what you are going to say. Note your questions. If you are giving instructions, pay attention to how you give them.
- Are you genuinely inviting participation, or are you really asking for a rubber stamp on what you have already decided?

Example

In a one-week planning workshop, a facilitator worked with a different group each day. In one group, he noticed that whenever the leader made a comment, it was to affirm what someone had just said or to make a very appropriate positive and encouraging suggestion, such as "We could do this idea at the same time we are doing this event" or "It would be possible for us to adjust our schedule in this way."

The following day he was in a group whose leader from time to time would get him aside and say, "What's the matter with these people? Why aren't they thinking about X? Why haven't they generated more data about Y?" The facilitator suggested the leader introduce his concerns in a manner conducive to group empowerment, such as by asking, "Have you considered X?" or "When does Y fit into your total plan?"

❧23❧

TV News Spot

Participation is perhaps the surest way to inspire commitment. Participation in planning and decision-making leads to ownership, and that in turn builds the commitment that is a prerequisite for excellence in workmanship.

—Spencer (1989)

Description

In order to give people a feel for pulling off an event, to help bridge gaps among team members, and to call forth a different level of participation from team members, I ask them to choose one of the activities that is already in their plan and create a three-minute TV news spot reporting on its successful completion. After the presentations, I ask a couple of processing questions to help them think through what has just happened.

Spontaneous creativity using both the left and the right brain can call forth unique skills and talents that are normally not seen in a typical meeting. (The left brain is considered to be the more logical and rational part; the right brain, the more creative and intuitive.) During the presentations by small teams, incredible appreciation is generated for the creativity and talents of everyone involved. This activity lays a foundation for appreciation of others' ideas and appreciation of the opportunity for full participation. Because of its potential for creating connections among people, it is a tool for creating consensus down the road.

Did You Know?

- An opportunity for creativity not only calls forth participation but provides a moment of bonding and connecting.
- Standing in the "victory circle" builds momentum and confidence to complete the project.
- In doing this activity, others can become as excited about your project as you are.

Activity: TV News Spot

1. Use the teams or the miniteams that are already part of your group.

2. After they have done some planning for the activities they are going to do during the coming year, have each team choose one activity or planned event.

3. Suggest they create a three-minute TV news spot to report on the occurrence of the event or the successful completion of the project.

4. Give everyone ten minutes to create their news spot.

5. Have each team give its presentation.

6. Applaud and recognize the efforts of each team after its presentation.

7. Allow time for one or two processing questions:
   a. How did your team work together?
   b. What did you learn?
   c. What really happened during this news spot exercise?

Hints

- You might have a few creative materials, such as colored paper, scissors, glue, cards, and markers, available for people to use in creating props.
- This simple strategy has many benefits. First, dramatizing the power of events and happenings indirectly suggests to the team that events and clear-cut accomplishments create excitement and motivation, not long, drawn-out committees or projects that take years and years.
- One of the other impacts of this activity is the breaking down of barriers among team members. People get to look at each other in a new light as they watch each other create this news spot.

Example

Leading a conference for businesspeople and local educators, I decided to insert this activity just before they did some serious planning. They had already laid out several possible highly motivating events. Each team had a mix of teachers and businesspeople.

The presentations were humorous and informative, representing a real belief that something important could be created. Creativity ran rampant. Someone found a mop in the hotel to use as a microphone. Many "hams" had a chance to shine.

During the processing conversation, I asked what happened. Many businesspeople said, "I had no idea how professional our teachers are. They really know about teaching." Likewise, the teachers said, "We had no idea how much these businesspeople care about the future of our community and our children." Barriers were broken down in a short amount of time.

≈24≈

Questions Not Dictums

> *It can be taken for granted that most organization members want to participate as fully and productively as possible, and that something blocks this happening.*

—Blake, Mouton, and Allen (1987)

Description

Open-ended questions are critical to generating the total participation of the group. A question that genuinely calls for true responses is one of the foundations of initiating participation. The phrasing of the question makes a difference. "What do you think about the proposed solution?" is not as helpful as "What are some possible solutions to this issue?" The effective leader's time is often better spent devising the most accurate and inviting questions than worrying about the answers needed.

Although many meetings consist of hearing reports from various teams and offering suggestions or comments on these reports, other meetings are held to discuss an issue or come up with some solutions to concerns. This is the kind of situation that can benefit from some real participation. It is at this point that the right question is crucial. The right question defines the concern but does not predict the "right" solution in its phrasing.

Did You Know?

- Like it or not, few people today want to be told exactly what to do.
- Questions invite; dictums turn people off.
- Questions communicate that you need help.
- Questions convey the truth: You do not have all the answers.

Activity: Questions Not Dictums

1. Write down all the concerns and issues for your next meeting.

2. Sort through these and choose only the ones that must be dealt with at this meeting.

3. Your skill as a leader is discerning what really has to be worked on in your meeting.

4. Get clarity on the real issue and the meeting product that will most help you relative to this issue.

5. Use this thinking to help you frame the open-ended question that really invites answers from the group.

6. Think through how you want the answers to be given. Is this an informal conversation? Will a brainstorm list be helpful? Is this the kind of question that calls for a full workshop, using the 5 × 8 cards referred to in Activity 7? The advantage of cards is that you can cluster and group them so that you can begin to see similarities in the responses to your question.

7. Again, be sure to allow time for processing, using one or two of these questions:
   a. What was helpful about our time together?
   b. What questions still remain for us?
   c. What are the next steps we need to take?

Hints

- During the brainstorm process, your role is affirmation. Every answer has merit and helps the group come to a solution. As a leader, your imagination is called on at all times to see the gift in the responses offered.
- Needless to say, while you are leading, it may not appear that every answer is worthwhile. But to foster the process and to keep the ball rolling in people's minds, ongoing affirmation is crucial. Continually discerning the group wisdom rather than responding negatively to what seems like an off-the-wall response takes a great deal of discipline. Possibly responding here with "John, say a little more about that" can reveal some hidden good idea.
- If several answers in a row seem off target, it may be because the whole group is still unclear about the intent of the question. When this happens, gently repeat or rephrase the question. Usually that is enough to generate some on-target responses.

Example

The Dictum column gives you examples of some dictums that undermine participation. The Question column illustrates questions that invite dialogue and creative thinking.

DICTUM	QUESTION
Tell me how you like this plan I've prepared.	What are some elements of a plan that will work for us?
This is how I want you to get this project done.	This is what we need accomplished. How might we get this done?
This is the way it's always been done.	Who has some ideas on more effective ways to get this done?
You've got to find ways to cut the cost of this.	What are some ways you've thought of to cut the cost of this?

⁓25⁓

Carousel Solutions

Inclusive solutions are wise solutions. Their wisdom emerges from the integration of everybody's perspectives and needs.

—Kaner (1996)

Description

This activity is another way to tap the wisdom of almost everyone in a group. It generates a lot of ideas and possibilities that can be pared down to workable ones at a later time.

Did You Know?

- One person's ideas often spark other ideas that would never have come out except for the idea of the first person.
- Different issues block different people. This activity capitalizes on the wisdom and thinking of a whole group and demonstrates that every situation has possible solutions.

Activity: Carousel Solutions

1. Clarify the facets of the issue or concern. This may require a brainstorm and pull-together through a list or through Cardstorming (Activity 7).

2. Once the facets of the issue have been named, write each one on a piece of chart paper.

3. Post the pieces of chart paper around the room.

4. Have groups of three or four gather around each piece of chart paper.

5. Ask each group to brainstorm solutions for its particular facet of the issue, recording the solutions on the paper.

6. After two or three minutes, ask every group to move clockwise to the next piece of chart paper. Give the groups two or three minutes to brainstorm about this facet of the issue and write down their ideas.

7. Shift the groups again, giving a minute or two for each of the remaining pieces of chart paper.

8. When each group has returned to its original piece of chart paper, have each group read the brainstorm of solutions.

9. Have each group come up with its recommendation for the top three or four ways to address its facet of the issue.

10. Have each group report.

11. Document the reports.

12. Ask for reflections on what has been useful about this process.

Hints

- Have each group use a different colored marker in case any of the brainstormed items needs to be clarified.
- It is important that some of the solutions that result from this activity actually get implemented, or the group will not trust a participatory process like this the next time.

Example

A middle school had a huge percentage of special needs students. The teachers were becoming overwhelmed even though many of them had special education training. The staff brainstormed all the manifestations of the problem that made it difficult for them to teach. They then categorized these into seven basic clusters of issues and concerns. The group divided into seven teams, and each team took one of the issue clusters and wrote a paragraph clarifying exactly what was going on in that issue. At the next meeting, seven sheets of chart paper were posted around the room, each one naming one of the issues. Each team began at one of the seven charts, brainstorming ways to address that particular issue or concern. After two or three minutes, the teams shifted clockwise. This happened again and again until they were back at their original issue. A representative of each team read the solutions. Everything was documented and distributed to each teacher. Each teacher now had seven to ten practical ideas for addressing each issue.

Chapter 5

Organizing the Meeting Focus: Things That Take Effort

INTRODUCTION TO FOCUS

Many meetings fall flat because the organizer has not done the preparation and homework ahead of time to guarantee an effective and time-efficient meeting. If a one-hour meeting is scheduled, then one hour's worth of business needs to be planned. Many times we insert five hours' worth of agenda into a one-hour meeting. This sets the meeting up for failure at the outset. Conversely, we may expect the meeting to run itself or just happen, and consequently we plan nothing. Meeting focus means clarity about the exact work to be accomplished, that is, clarity about the products that can realistically be expected from the amount of time scheduled.

You can't have a clear idea of the participative processes you want to use until you are clear about what you want the meeting to accomplish. Many unfocused meetings joined with haphazard participative processes have given participative processes a bad name.

When this occurs, distrust for the effectiveness of team collaboration grows. Consequently, trust in consensus diminishes.

The leader then resorts to tried-and-true methods for making decisions and getting the job done. The organizer blames the team when in actuality the organizer's own poor meeting coordination is at fault. A clear focus that promises meeting accomplishments and enables them to happen is more critical than people realize in creating an atmosphere in which consensus can grow confidently.

If the meeting agenda continually seems overwhelming and overcrowded, you may need to break the group down into smaller teams that will bring recommendations about the agenda items to the full group. Using smaller teams would replace the time for a whole-group discussion with a conversation by just two or three people, saving whole-group discussion for concrete recommendations.

The activities in this section can all help you, the leader, organize a more effective meeting.

∽26∾

One Concrete Product

The manager role is to reach inside each employee and release his unique talents into performance.

—Buckingham and Coffman (1999)

Description

The organizer decides beforehand what concrete products are going to come out of the meeting. They could include a major decision about a current concern, a list of possible options relative to a major decision, an update on what is happening, or the responses to a particularly controversial situation. The organizer thinks through what the team can reasonably expect to accomplish in the time available. The push of this activity is that there be at least one visible, concrete product that people immediately recognize as the goal of the meeting. Meetings that go on and on with no visible product bring morale down quickly. Likewise, meetings with ten major, concrete product goals paralyze those attending.

Bad meetings do not just happen. Their planners have usually ignored critical guidelines. Just encouraging a participative process does not fulfill your duties as the organizer or planner. Choosing exactly what needs to come out of the meeting and mapping out the most helpful participative process to get your team there are tasks requiring leadership skill.

Did You Know?

- Two short, well-organized meetings might be more efficient than one long meeting.
- If your team is made up of eight people and you meet for one hour, you are using the resource of eight person hours.
- Meetings without any visible products drive people crazy.

Activity: One Concrete Product

This activity is one you do yourself before the meeting.

1. List all the items that come to mind for the agenda.

2. Ask others on the team before the meeting for concerns or items they may have for the agenda.

3. Screen these items by asking yourself these questions:
   a. Which of these absolutely must be dealt with at this meeting?
   b. Which of these need some more small-team work to be ready for a fruitful full-team discussion?
   c. If we did put this on the agenda, what is the expected result of the whole team's looking at it?
   d. Is this an item a small team needs to talk through, returning to the next meeting with a set of recommendations?
   e. Is this an item that belongs with our team?
   f. If this issue is complicated, what piece of its resolution can actually be handled at this meeting?

4. Separate your items into Quick Items, Major Items, and Minor Items.

5. Put two or three of the Quick Items at the beginning of the agenda. Coming to rapid decisions at the front end of the meeting will provide some motivation for the team.

6. While the team is still fresh, choose to deal with the Major Items. Keeping to the time flow is critical here.

7. Wrapping up the meeting with some work on Minor Items should go fairly easily since the team will have already dealt with the most difficult items.

Hints

- The skill here is determining what actually has to occur at the meeting. Certain agenda items can be accomplished outside the regular meeting. Other agenda items need some work before they are fully ready for the meeting.
- Knowing exactly what product you need relative to each minor issue is just as critical as knowing what product you need on each major issue.
- Most meetings restrict themselves to one major product. You will lose effectiveness if a group has to wrestle through one difficult issue after another. Furthermore, you lose efficiency if the whole group has to hash out everything from start to finish instead of using small groups to do much of the hashing out before the meeting even begins.
- Watching the dynamics is important. If a resolution does not emerge, is something more needed? Are people worn out? Is there another time the final decision could be made? Is it time to point out what pieces have been resolved as a way to move people toward a resolution? Has enough discussion taken place that two or three people could be asked to step aside for ten to fifteen minutes to refine a recommendation while the full group works on some of the minor items? As a facilitator, you have many options for how to progress.
- The most debilitating thing about meetings is the sense that time is being wasted. A frequent comment is, "We spent all this time and did not accomplish a thing." Generally, people do not begrudge time itself, but they do begrudge wasted time.

Example

Here is a sample of the kinds of meeting agenda items that might fall into each of the three categories.

QUICK ITEMS	MAJOR ITEMS	MINOR ITEMS
Team reports from the previous week	Major policy decisions	Revamping project timeline
Information updates	Creation of a 6-month plan	Shifting task responsibilities
Reports on shifts in company policy	Important budget revisions	Choosing project dates

∾27∾

Time Flow Picture

Conventional wisdom suggests that effectiveness comes from a strong leader, a clear mission, and technically competent subordinates. Yet more is involved if a team is to realize synergy. The key issue is in how the parts act together—participation.

—Blake, Mouton, and Allen (1987)

Description

A Time Flow Picture is simply a visual layout of the meeting. I recommend that before the meeting starts, the facilitator lay out the flow of the meeting in a simple visual image, to be presented at the very beginning of the meeting.

Many leaders often prepare a list of the agenda items and pass this out ahead of time. This is very helpful in that it demonstrates some thinking about what needs to happen at the meeting. Often, however, an agenda list gives no sense of priority, nor does it suggest the actual flow of time.

An agenda list of twenty items for a designated meeting time of ninety minutes communicates immediately that there is no realistic expectation of making the ninety-minute time frame. Morale plummets. People need to believe that it is possible to accomplish the agenda within the stated time frame. A time flowchart can communicate that agenda goals are within reach.

Did You Know?

- Because people feel so pressed about time and schedules, their anxieties are reduced when they see a clear picture of the time flow.
- Some people feel time is a more precious commodity than money.
- Since every one of us has the same amount of time—168 hours every week—our only question is how best to use the time we are given.

Activity: Time Flow Picture

1. Write down all the components and elements of your meeting.

2. Make an initial layout of the flow from beginning to end (see Activity 26, One Concrete Product, for one way to do this).

3. Lay the components of the meeting across your timeline so that you can see both the order and the time allotment for each item.

4. Check for feasibility.

5. Make a visual representation of your proposed time flow to present to your team at your next meeting.

MEETING FLOW		
Introduction 2 min.		
Quick items	Major items	Minor items
10 min.	30 min.	16 min.
Conclusion 2 min.		

Hints

- Try to be honest about exactly how long each component will take to accomplish. That will help you create a time flow picture that is realistic.
- I use small sticky notes to lay out the elements I want to cover in the meeting. Then I rearrange them on my desk until I get the flow that makes sense to me.
- It is often difficult to start when only four of your ten team members have arrived on time. How can you proceed if only 40% of your team is there? Although there are times when it is necessary to wait, waiting teaches the 40% to come late next time, initiating a trend toward starting later and later. When I plan a meeting, I start with a conversation or a short activity to set the stage. It is usually quite enjoyable but not crucial to the content of the whole meeting. This lets me start the meeting on time and still allow for some people to arrive late.

Example

A leader was once in charge of training a group of people in complex finance procedures for a major project. His sessions typically looked like the following:

TRAINING SESSION FLOW		
Introduction		
Where we are on project timeline—THE BIG PICTURE		
		2 min.
Quick Items	**Major Items**	**Minor Items**
Review and polishing last meeting's major product	Training session on next phase of finance procedures	Content of team report to department meeting
		Minor task realignments
12 min.	25 min.	15 min.
Conclusion		
Processing question: What worked well for us in today's session? 3 min.		

≈28≈

Meeting Space

The effective, or ineffective, use of space at a meeting locale can exert a subtle yet powerful influence on the mood of participants and the ability of the group to focus its attention on the issues.

—Spencer (1989)

Description

The physical layout of meeting space is more important than we often realize. How you place the tables and chairs can communicate a great deal to the participants in the meeting. It is crucial to know ahead of time what the space looks like so that you can arrange it to enhance the participation of your team.

In some spaces, such as most board of education or town council meeting rooms, the board or council members sit on a raised dais, separating them from the public. They have tables, and the public does not. This arrangement communicates that only the board or council is to have any significant impact on decisions. Theater-style room arrangements have everyone facing the platform or stage. This arrangement also communicates that all the action and decision making will take place at a level above the group members. A room full of tables and chairs communicates that everyone is a participant.

Although a room needs a focus (such as the front), it also needs a way for interaction to occur. Fostering both focus and interaction can be tricky.

Did You Know?

- Neat table and chair arrangement communicates that the meeting has a plan.
- Too many extra chairs around the table lowers the mood because it communicates that you expected many more people.

Activity: Meeting Space

Here are things to review as you plan the layout of your meeting space.

1. Decide the best working wall for the meeting (i.e., where the chart paper or 5×8 cards are going to go up).

2. Arrange the tables so that people sitting at both the long sides can see the front. Or, if people are not going to spend much time in separate teams or subgroups, tables can be connected, as shown below.

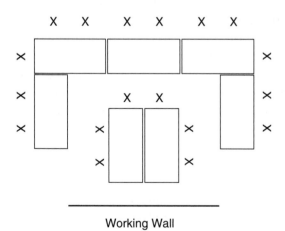

Working Wall

3. If you intend for work in teams to take up a lot of meeting time, arrange your tables into separate team tables, as shown below.

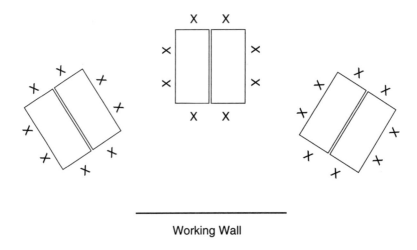

Working Wall

Hints

- Unless you are very spatially gifted, there is no substitute for showing up early at the meeting space and checking it out. Very often even a little rearrangement can make a difference.
- I often discover that while most people want to set up a meeting to face the obvious front, creating the focus along a side wall gives more wall work space and allows more people to be closer to the working wall.
- Since the focus is on the working wall, the first set of tables can be as close as two or three feet from the wall.
- Pay attention to the suggestions of people working with you. Other people may see space options more quickly than you do.

Example

A facilitator held an all-day workshop in a school auditorium, complete with theater-style seats and no tables. None of the classrooms were big enough to hold all the people who were to attend the planning workshop. Finally the group decided to use the cafeteria. The tables were designed for eating and had benches attached to them. However, one side wall in the cafeteria was completely blank. It worked perfectly. It was easy to arrange the tables so that everyone could sit around a table and see the working wall.

∽29∾

Materials

The most effective meetings result in a meaningful, and ideally, tangible product. . . . A product that documents the decision or plan arrived at by the group reminds members of the group's consensus and serves as a guide for future action and progress evaluations.

—Spencer (1989)

Description

Because you want a tangible product, often tangible materials are needed for your meeting. Preparing the necessary materials beforehand further communicates how seriously you consider the time and participation of the people attending. Having everything at your fingertips creates a smooth meeting flow. Bringing the various materials and procuring enough of them enables you to keep the meeting moving toward its goal.

People feel they have been thought about and cared for when all the materials necessary are present for a meeting. This preparation communicates that you feel the meeting is important. It is one more element that supports an atmosphere that leads to consensus.

Did You Know?

- Simple, adequate materials reduce the time wasted and increase the team members' confidence.
- Even adults enjoy using markers of varying colors.

- Creating a visible product during a team meeting gives people a great sense of accomplishment.

Activity: Materials

This is another activity that requires your thought ahead of time and that enables your meeting to keep to its focus.

1. Ahead of time, look at the flow of your meeting.
2. List the materials you will need for each section of the meeting.
3. Place them close to where you stand or sit during the meeting.
4. Keep them somewhere readily available for succeeding meetings.

Hints

- Some facilitators like to keep their materials together in a box they always bring to the meeting.
- Looking at each piece of the meeting flow is crucial as different materials are often required for different sections of a meeting. In fact, one way to help the flow of a meeting is to use different methods or approaches for each section.
- A brainstorm may need chart paper, markers, and masking tape. A full workshop might need 5 × 8 cards, markers, and masking tape. Decision making might require chart paper, markers, and masking tape to work through the various options. Some activities are enhanced if different colors of markers are available. Other activities need a special form on which people can write down their responses.

Example

Sample materials list:

chart paper	easel with paper
masking tape	markers of assorted colors

5 × 8 cards	scratch paper (recycled paper)
sticky notes	folders
scissors	stapler and staples
ruler	correction fluid
note paper	pens and pencils

While you are planning your meeting, you can add materials to your time flow picture. Below is the time flow picture from Activity 27 (Time Flow Picture) with materials added.

TRAINING SESSION FLOW			
Introduction			
Where we are on project timeline—THE BIG PICTURE 2 min.			
	Quick Items	**Major Items**	**Minor Items**
A G E N D A	Reviewing and polishing last meeting's major product 12 min.	Training session on next phase of finance procedures 25 min.	Content of team report to department meeting Minor task realignments 15 min.
M A T E R I A L S	Typed product— copies for all	Chart paper Markers Tape Sample exercises	5 × 8 cards Markers Tape task assignment sheets
Conclusion			
Processing question: What worked well for us in today's session? 3 min.			

⁓30⁓

Meeting Plan Forms

*It is up to the leader to carry out these processes compe-
tently and in a manner that is responsive to people's
needs.*

—Nelson and Burns (in Adams, 1984)

Description

For almost every meeting I plan, I use a simple meeting
plan form to help me organize my thoughts and think about
how I want the meeting to flow. This form is a guideline, not
a rigid prescription. A meeting form is a tool for focusing your
attention on the meeting at hand. Knowing you are going to
fill out the meeting form helps you concentrate on the meeting. Also, some meetings may get unexpectedly complicated.
Having your plan in front of you can help you keep on track.

I have discovered that the written plan helps me be more
flexible. As long as I have made it through the main action or
product, I can cut others short or postpone them until a future
meeting. Without going through the prioritizing and planning, I might find it much harder to be flexible in figuring out
how to shorten something, cut it out, or postpone it.

Did You Know?

- It may take you more than one hour to carefully plan a
  one-hour meeting.

- Time spent after the meeting to think about what went well and how to improve your meetings is as valuable as the time you spend beforehand planning the meeting.
- Because a printed agenda is like a road map through your meeting, you want to make it easy to follow.

Activity: Meeting Plan Forms

1. Note all the items you have decided to include in the meeting you are planning.

2. Using the meeting plan form, put your agenda items into the appropriate places.

3. The plan form has a place for the Meeting Objective and the Experiential Goal. The Meeting Objective is the primary goal or objective for the meeting—the most important thing you want to accomplish or the primary item you want people to know after the meeting. The Experiential Goal is what you want people to experience and feel by the end of the meeting. I find these to be critical guidelines in deciding what the meeting is about.

4. I conclude with one or more processing questions. The purpose of these is to help the team step back from the content of the meeting and think together about what has been going on—either the content or the methods being used. It is a great opportunity, as openness increases, to get some feedback on the team members' sense of the meeting. Choose one or more of these processing questions:
   a. What has been important to you about this meeting?
   b. What do you like about what we have been doing?
   c. What don't you like? Why?
   d. What are your suggestions as to how we might proceed next?
   e. What methods seem to be working for us?

f. What approaches do not seem to be working for us?

g. What other methods or approaches do you think we should try?

Hints

- As I mentioned earlier, I often jot down the elements of the meeting on small sticky notes. Then I place the stickies in the appropriate slots on my meeting plan form so I can arrange and rearrange them easily. When I am satisfied with the way it looks, I fill out the form.
- Sometimes I use pencil on the form so that I can change or add things easily.
- I also find it helpful to make this plan at least a day ahead of time. Very often when I wake up on the day of the meeting, ideas suddenly come that help me polish and fine-tune my planning of the day or night before.

Example

Note that this form is a little more detailed and complex than the ones used in Activities 27 and 29.

MEETING PLAN FORM				
Introduction	**Meeting Objective**		**Experiential Goal**	
Remind people why this community input meeting is so important.	For the team to come up with a plan for a community input meeting on alternative time/calendar options for school day/year		Heightened confidence on the team members' part that they can pull off this meeting well	
	Agenda			
Purpose	**Quick Items**	**Major Issues**	**Minor Issues**	**Processing**
Quick conversation: What do we want the hallmarks of this meeting to be?	Who do we want to attend this meeting? Where will it be held? When shall we hold it?	What elements need to be part of this meeting? Discern main points of agreement. Lay out time flow.	Who will lead this meeting? What tasks need to be done to get ready for this meeting?	Ask one or two of these questions: What went well? Where did we struggle? Where did we come together and focus well as a group?
Materials	Chart paper Tape Markers	5 × 8 cards Markers Chart paper Tape	Chart paper Tape Markers	
Conclusion	Next meeting date and time			

Chapter 6

Tapping the Group Agreement: For the Committed

INTRODUCTION TO AGREEMENT

Tapping the group agreement involves participative methods and processes to discern where the group agreement currently is. It also means constantly clarifying to the group what it currently has said yes to. The difficult aspect of this stage is that it goes far beyond merely taking a vote to see if a majority agrees on something. Tapping the group agreement is about discerning which elements of a given topic the whole group is willing to run with and which ones the group is not ready to go with yet.

When I am facilitating, I work hard to avoid a situation calling for a vote. In the very beginning of the life of a group, votes may be difficult to avoid. However, beyond such decisions as where to eat lunch, I avoid votes because they divide a group into two camps. Voting reveals the group's disagreements rather than enhancing or clarifying its agreements. Instead, you can try at every point to create options and solutions that the whole group can affirm. Approaches that reveal the group agreement are at the very heart of the consensus-building process.

Tapping the group agreement is one of the most difficult arenas of participation because it requires the most from the facilitator and relies so heavily on the facilitator's intuition. Can the group move on, or does it need to spend more time on an issue? Because this aspect of participation often relies heavily on the judgment of the facilitator, it is the hardest to manage while still guarding the participative processes. Thus the facilitator needs great skill to reveal to the group its current thinking, options, and level of consensus.

⪻31⪼

Guidelines for a Consensus Outcome

In order for a group to reach a sustainable agreement, the members need to understand and accept the legitimacy of one another's needs and goals.

—Kaner (1996)

Description

This activity is especially helpful for a group that has not had much experience in consensus. This activity asks that before a group does much concrete work on a decision it needs to make, it consider what the crucial elements of that decision would be, regardless of what decision is reached. In other words, what guidelines or criteria would any solution need to satisfy?

Did You Know?

- Agreement on these guidelines could very possibly pave the way for consensus on the decision.
- This activity very helpfully projects people into the future, setting the stage for all the dialogue to follow.

Activity: Guidelines for a Consensus Outcome

1. Divide the group into pairs or triads.
2. Ask people to think individually about guidelines and criteria for the decision the group needs to make.

3. Then have them share in pairs or triads.

4. Have each pair or triad share one of its guidelines.

5. Add to the list anything not said yet.

6. Go over the list and polish, combine, or delete (a list of more than 10 guidelines becomes awkward to deal with).

7. Document the guidelines and post them throughout the process.

Hints

- You might categorize these guidelines into bottom-line guidelines, which must be met, and bonus guidelines, which would be advantageous to meet.
- Instead of the workshop format suggested in the steps section, this activity could also be done as an informal conversation, which might come across as less threatening, paving the way for more agreement because it is done in a more relaxed tone.
- The dialogue at every point in this activity can be very revealing—not only about what is underneath what people are saying but about what is not being said.

Example

A committee of school and community representatives was charged with finding a solution to the school's problem of overcrowding. Very early on the facilitator worked with the members to lay out what the guidelines and criteria would be for any decision they made. These guidelines actually became the first consensus event for this committee. The group stuck with them, and they provided real guidance for future proceedings.

∽32∾

Workshop Flow

Postindustrial technology has also become so complex that it's impossible for managers to have all the answers.

—Spencer (1989)

Description

When your intent is to gather the ideas of a group of people and help the group see what its thinking and agreement are, these five steps are critical: Context, Idea Gathering, Organizing, Clarifying, and Processing. They carefully guide the leader and the group to consensus and incorporate individual thinking and group dialogue in the process.

Did You Know?

- Getting and using participation is a highly structured process.
- Agreement does not come naturally to people raised on rugged individualism.
- A facilitator controls the process but not the content.

Activity: Workshop Flow

Context

1. Set the stage. Remind people of the reason for this particular workshop.

2. State the real question (see Activity 19) or the particular focus of this workshop.

3. Remind people of the major steps of the process: Context, Idea Gathering, Organizing, Clarifying, and Processing.

Idea Gathering

1. Allow people time to think through their own responses individually.

2. Have people talk through their ideas in groups of three or four.

Organizing

1. Get the ideas on chart paper or 5 × 8 cards (see Activities 3 and 7).

2. As in Activity 3, if your list is on chart paper, have the group intuitively discern the major clusters the data fall in.

3. If you are using cards, after getting the cards up front, do the clustering and the naming of temporary titles described in Activity 7.

Clarifying

1. Review and polish the temporary titles by making sure each temporary title still identifies what the cluster is about.

2. Then elicit two or three adjectives that make the title crystal clear. *Funding* tells you the arena. *Diverse, Dependable Funding* tells you much more accurately what the group wants. Remember that this is the stage in which real group agreement occurs. The discussions about these titles form the real consensus.

Processing

Choose one or two of the following questions and pose them to the group:

1. Content Processing
   a. Which cluster speaks most to you in terms of your daily work?
   b. Which cluster gets you most excited and intrigued?
   c. Which cluster will have the most impact on the organization?
   d. What have we accomplished?
   e. What are some implications of the work we have done today?

2. Method Processing
   a. What methods or steps seemed to work for us today?
   b. Where did you get most involved?
   c. How could you use something like this in another situation?

Hints

- Be sure to allow people time to do individual thinking first.
- You can pursue some of the implications in greater detail by asking what next steps or decisions need to be made.
- As the leader, you are often tempted to comment on some of the data presented. Needless to say, the fewer comments you make, the better. Value judgments about any of the responses are unnecessary as you seek the points of agreement revealed in the cluster titles.

Example

It often happens that people see this workshop a few times and then go right out and use it in their own work settings.

After a series of workshops for the flight attendant division of an airline company, the two top division managers proceeded to hold input meetings throughout the country, using this workshop flow with thousands of flight attendants. They reported that the high quality of the input genuinely informed their continued planning and policy decisions. The five-step framework really worked for them.

⁓33⁓

Three-to-One Scenarios

*In companies that make things happen today . . . employ-
ees are seen as the company's most important resource in
meeting the challenge of change.*

—Spencer (1989)

Description

When a group understands an issue clearly and is ready to
map out some solutions, it can divide into three teams to create scenarios about the critical pieces of the solution. Having
each team present its own scenario will help the group discern
the elements of winning solutions. When writing their scenario, teams may also discover elements that may not be
appropriate or workable. Out of three possible scenarios, the
group can then create one winning solution, perhaps with elements from all three scenarios.

The key work of the teams is to pull the elements of a possible solution together into a scenario. In other words, each
team is charged with writing the script or plot of one possible
solution to the issue and satisfying the criteria previously
identified by the group.

Did You Know?

- The journey to consensus begins with small steps of
  agreement.

- Helping people see a variety of options actually helps them see the direction they really want to go.
- Seeing a variety of options helps clarify the criteria a group has for a desired solution.

Activity: Three-to-One Scenarios

1. Divide the group into three teams.

2. Charge each team with coming up with a scenario that would satisfy the constraints of the situation.

3. Have each team record its scenario on a piece of chart paper.

4. Have each team present its scenario. Recognize each team with a round of applause.

5. Have the group process all the presentations together by asking one or two of the following questions:
   a. Which aspects of these scenarios stand out to you?
   b. Which one(s) interest you the most?
   c. Where do you see some connections or common elements in the scenarios?
   d. Where are the major differences?
   e. What are the implications of each of these scenarios?
   f. How would you characterize each one or title each one?
   g. As you look through all these together, what seem to be elements of the one winning solution?

6. Put the winning elements on 5 × 8 cards or on a piece of chart paper.

7. Keep working with the elements until the pieces and the flow of the winning solution come into focus.

8. Suggest that this one winning solution stand for a few minutes or a few days so that the team can come back to it, examine it, and polish it.

9. Process how the group currently feels about the winning solution. Check whether there are any major gaps or holes in the winning solution.

10. Conclude the activity with one or two final processing questions:
    a. What steps in this process seemed to work especially well for us?
    b. What aspects of this product are you particularly pleased with?
    c. What happened to us as a group while we worked on this?
    d. In what kind of situation could you use this process again?

Hints

- It is very helpful to have some data or additional information about other people's possible solutions.
- As they begin, many groups may feel tremendous uncertainty about creating a scenario. Allow the groups to experience that ambiguity fully so that they may also experience a breakthrough.
- If possible, allow some time to pass between initially creating the winning solution and finishing the product. Even waiting one day allows the group to get some distance, enhance the solution, deal with any inconsistencies, and attain buy-in. Very often people react negatively until they have a chance to absorb the full impact of the solution and think it through for themselves.

Example

A school advisory group was trying to find a solution to an emotionally charged issue. The group had already received input from five community focus groups, one teacher focus group, several classes, and a local school council meeting.

The whole group took the data and identified all the possible solution pieces or elements. Then using these as "ingredients for a recipe," so to speak, each team chose various pieces or elements and created a solution scenario.

After each team presented its scenario, the group fashioned a winning solution with elements from each of the team scenarios.

≈34≈

Cooperative Writing Workshop

As they begin to feel that they and their ideas really make a difference to the company, passive workers become actively engaged in the creative change process.

—Spencer (1989)

Description

This activity enables a group of people to write a full document in teams in such a way that the final product has flow and continuity. The final product often impresses the group with its comprehensiveness and unity. After experiencing the successful completion of this cooperative writing activity, many people realize their group is more connected than they thought.

The key to this activity is dividing both the document and the group into workable parts. For example, fifteen people could make five teams of three, which also suggests dividing the document into five pieces.

Did You Know?

- Writing about the group's points of consensus helps a group connect the points of agreement and deepen the foundation of its consensus.
- Once a group has a common experience of creating points of consensus, its writing is amazingly consistent.

- Writing about the group's points of consensus is a structured format that enables the group to get penetrating clarity about its thinking.

Activity: Cooperative Writing Workshop

1. After a group has experienced something like a workshop or input of data, you may have the group do some writing together.

2. If the group has not already created the structure of the document to be written, hold a workshop to create the actual structure of the document itself. Very often after I lead a workshop on purposeful vision (Activity 17), the group wants to write a mission statement built on the elements identified in that workshop.

3. Suggest to the group a common structure to each piece of the document, such as an introduction, a definition of the piece, some examples of what the piece is about, some of its implications, and finally a word about its significance or importance.

4. You might even prepare ahead of time a form that each team could use in writing its section.

5. Divide the group into the same number of teams as the document will have sections.

6. Suggest a reasonable time limit, from twenty minutes for a paragraph to several days for a chapter-length assignment.

7. If the document is short enough, have the teams read their section aloud in its entirety. If the document is too long, have each team read samples of its writing. Find an appropriate way to recognize each team's contribution.

8. After the reading, pose one or two of the following questions to allow the group to step back and process what it has heard:

a. What did you notice about the document we created?
b. What words or phrases did you appreciate?
c. What intrigued or surprised you?
d. As a whole, what are some of the major ideas this document communicates?
e. What are our next steps with this document?

Hints

- I would do this activity only if the group has some common experience, such as a workshop, on which to base its writing. Otherwise the writing may sound as if it comes from conflicting and contradictory perspectives.
- When the group has shared a workshop or some other kind of common experience, the group is able to write with smooth flow and continuity.

Example

A commission on a small city council had amassed a 300-page document representing its plans for some major rehabilitation in the downtown area. The group was concerned that people had lost the sense of what the whole planning effort was about. First the facilitator led a workshop like the vision workshop described in Activity 17 to capture the components of the vision to be outlined in the document. Then the group wrote a summary paragraph about each of the eight major elements of its vision. The initial workshop and the writing took less than two hours altogether.

When the members heard the summary document they had written, they were astounded. Many commented that it was only then that they understood all the work they had been doing.

⇒35⇐

Mapping the Road to Agreement

Workers who contribute their input to a plan feel pride of ownership. They become committed to the plan's success and see themselves as integral to its execution.

—Spencer (1989)

Description

There are times when a group is just not ready to come to agreement. When you have the option of a little more time and can schedule a follow-up meeting, you can conclude the workshop by asking, "What do we need to settle in order to come to an agreement?" or "What are the items we need more clarity about before this group can reach an agreement?" Then teams can be created to handle each major item with the understanding that they will come to the next meeting with information or with a model that will lead the group to agreement.

When a group gets into a morass, the pathway to agreement is unclear. The facilitator can use the group's own thinking to create the group's own pathway to agreement.

Did You Know?

- The solution to conflict lies within the group itself.
- The people closest to the conflict within the group are the very people who know the way to agreement.

- Seeing the stages on the road to agreement makes consensus feel more possible.

Activity: Mapping the Road to Agreement

Knowing when to use this activity is tricky. It is not to be used to help the group escape from the demands of coming to agreement. But if time permits, this activity is helpful when a group appears to be at an immense impasse. The strategy is an attempt to help the group grasp what is really standing in the way of some genuine agreement.

1. Begin by helping the group state its current points of agreement.

2. Help the group name the unsettled points.

3. If necessary, do Cardstorming or a brainstormed list (Activities 7 and 3, respectively) to identify what needs to be settled before the group can reach agreement. You may have only a few items. If you have several items, you will want to use the list or the cards to discern the major clusters of three to five larger issues.

4. Have the group form subteams to deal with those issues and come prepared with information or a model for agreement by the next meeting.

5. At the next meeting, have each group report.

6. By this time the group will have all the necessary information or clarity it needs to reach agreement. Perhaps the Three-to-One Scenarios activity (Activity 33) could be employed at this point.

Hints

- Small teams are important in this activity for pulling together some consensus within the small teams before coming back to the larger group. When a group reaches a morass, for some reason individuals become reluctant to compromise and come to consensus. This strategy allows them to reach a consensus in a small group first.

- Particularly with a group that has been functioning for some time, the facilitator needs to step back when a morass develops and figure out what is really blocking a consensus. Consensus building relies heavily on trust. It is always helpful for facilitators to ask themselves whether the main roadblock to consensus is a content issue or an issue of group dynamics. This strategy provides an opportunity for the next stage of trust to occur.

Example

A social service agency began a meeting with an assumption by a few that the agency should carry out a very controversial project that would definitely elicit hostile responses from the neighborhood. As the meeting progressed, it became clear that the whole group had not agreed to proceed with the controversial project. In fact, as the members spoke together, an alternative strategy began to emerge. Yet the original few were not ready to give up their controversial plan.

In order to come to agreement, the group needed to know what various constituencies would think about their new alternative strategies. One team was sent to find out which strategy the city council would support. Another was to find out which strategy the agency's clients would prefer. A third group was to check with members not present at the meeting. When the group reconvened two weeks later, overwhelming support for the less controversial strategy allowed everyone to come to agreement on which way to proceed.

∽36∽

Agreement: State and Restate

Effective participation results in a greater flow of ideas and positions and requires a sound means to deal with the differences that emerge.

—Blake, Mouton, and Allen (1987)

Description

From time to time, it is helpful to state the points of agreement so far. This reminds team members of the things they have agreed to say no to and the things they have agreed to say yes to. Furthermore, it is useful to clarify what they have not yet agreed on. It is helpful to remind a roadblocked group of the progress it has made already. Because groups experience difficulty perceiving their progress, a statement of where a group is always reveals the progress it is making.

Did You Know?

- Reminding people of where they have already created agreement encourages them to make the next step of agreement.
- Stating and restating exactly where a group is keeps it focused on the next step of agreement.
- Stating and restating points of agreement communicates to the group that you as the leader are paying close attention to everything that is going on.

Activity: Agreement: State and Restate

During the meeting in which you are seeking agreement, every few minutes state to the group exactly where it is in the whole process of coming to agreement.

1. If your group is doing something simple such as planning an agenda for a meeting, you can merely repeat the pieces that already have agreement and point out what is still unsettled: "So far we agree on the introduction, the presentation of data, and a time for questions. What we are not clear on yet is precisely which issue we want to get input about. What is your thinking now on that?"

2. If you are faced with something more difficult, however, such as trimming $500,000 from your budget, I would suggest two kinds of comments:

   "So far we have decided to save $100,000 by eliminating new purchases and $50,000 through a percentage cut of everyone's budget."

   Or

   "So far we have decided not to touch benefits, supplies, or salaries."

   And in either case, I would add the following:

   "Remember as we proceed, these are the six values and guidelines we have established for this whole budget-trimming process."

   I would also have chart paper up front to document both the decisions that have already been made, such as the $100,000 and $50,000 reductions, and the values and guidelines originally established to help the group through the process. Then I would say,

   "So what are some possible sources for the remaining $350,000?"

Hints

- You may find it helpful to use both visual and auditory reinforcements in this activity.
- The more complex the decisions, the more a group needs cues to remind it of where it has come from and where it is heading.
- You may need to implement some elements of Activity 35 (Mapping the Road to Agreement) before a final resolution can occur.

Example

A facilitator was invited to lead a workshop with a group that reportedly had two very divergent views about how to proceed. The first step was to clarify with them the one question both sides were trying to answer. Then the facilitator helped the group lay out visually the two clashing directions. By constantly stating and restating both the areas of agreement and the areas of disagreement, he got agreement on at least the common question, the two divergent solutions, and their implications. This meeting clarified the fact that one solution would save money in the short run but that the other solution would eventually have to be pursued anyway. The facilitator decided to use a second meeting to proceed further. In a few days, without the second meeting, he was surprised to hear that the second solution had been chosen with full agreement.

⧼37⧽

Testing for Consensus

Making a decision by consensus can take more time than other methods, but because people are then internally committed to the decision, it will usually take less time to implement effectively.

—Schwarz (2002)

Description

This activity occurs after a proposal has been suggested and various questions of clarity have been answered. It is a process for judging whether genuine consensus has been attained.

Did You Know?

- It is crucial to guard against "false consensus" or "hasty consensus." In false consensus, the group appears to have reached a consensus. In reality, there are people who have remained quiet and don't agree at all with the decision and have no intentions of supporting it.
- In hasty consensus, the group moves quickly to close the discussion and move on. There are people in the group who do not agree with the decision and will not support it because their concerns and reservations have not been dealt with adequately.

Activity: Testing for Consensus

1. Summarize the proposal or decision suggested.

2. Clarify what you are *not* asking, that is, you are not asking them to agree that this is the best proposal relative to their personal wishes. You are not asking them to agree that this is their first choice.

3. Clarify what you *are* asking, which is whether this proposal meets the guidelines set up before researching possible decisions. You are asking them to agree that this proposal represents the group's soundest deliberating at the moment. You are asking them whether they can live with this and support it.

4. The group may come to immediate agreement. Consensus has been attained.

5. The group may raise unresolved questions. Once these are resolved, the group comes to agreement. Consensus has been attained.

6. Some of the group members believe the guidelines have not all been met. After more discussion and perhaps modification of the proposal, the group feels the solution meets all the guidelines. Consensus has been attained.

7. The group is unable to come to agreement. Consensus has not been attained.

8. In the event consensus has not been attained, it is helpful to clarify the crucial remaining concerns or issues. The group may decide nothing more can be done. The group could ask three or four members to go back to the drawing board and prepare another proposal for the next meeting.

9. End with repeating the guidelines and restating the necessity of a proposal that addresses the original need.

Hints

- This activity can take the group into much discussion. It is important to state and restate the comments that are made to be sure everyone's insights are clear to the whole group.
- Sometimes just knowing one's insight has been accurately heard will open people up to compromise and acceptance.
- It is crucial to let the conversation flow until it is clear that the basic insights have been stated and heard.
- While it is tempting to just move on, a welcoming tone to additional insights conveys to the group that the leader is willing to listen to concerns and suggestions.

Example

Once it appears that consensus has been reached, a good facilitator states clearly what the consensus appears to be. A few seconds of silence are called for to let the consensus sink in. It doesn't take long for someone to offer a suggestion. When these suggestions come in, a good facilitator turns to the group for its response. Often a group immediately responds in the affirmative. Just as often, no one responds. In that case, the person who made the suggestion knows that the group heard it but didn't find it helpful. After an appropriate length of time, a good facilitator suggests what the consensus seems to be. If no one objects, consensus has been reached. If there is an objection, the facilitator works with the group some more, eventually stating what the new consensus is.

PART III

Individual Commitment

If a person does not feel this burning fire, you cannot light it for him.

A manager can never breathe motivational life into someone else. All she can do is try to identify each employee's striving four-lane highways and then, as far as is possible, cultivate these.

—Buckingham and Coffman (1999, p. 92)

I deas alone cannot fully link people together. What connects people is not mere ideas but deep personal commitments. Commitments involve feeling, passion, and drive. Ideas only bring heads together. The head is not the source of feeling, passion, and drive. When you feel someone else's commitment to something you also have committed to, you become connected to the other person with more than your head.

So how does real consensus happen? It begins at the commitment level. That person whose political party is different from mine is deeply committed to a safe environment in our community. I want that too. This other person whose management style is the opposite of mine desperately wants employee morale to increase. So do I. Connections grow. The potential for consensus rises when you discover that someone is deeply committed to that which you are committed to. You may even step back and examine that person's ideas from a new perspective. This examination of others' perspectives is critical for consensus because what genuinely drives and concerns people is often much more similar and concrete than mere ideology. When we begin to speak to each other out of our deep commitments, mutual respect grows, and energy for the task deepens.

This shared commitment can grow strong enough to shield and protect individuals in the midst of the stress and burdens of carrying out the group's tasks. It is as if the more you are reminded of the commitment of the group, the more ounces of energy you are able to squeeze out, and the more you are able to withstand any criticism or cynicism coming from outside the group. Individual commitment provides the stamina that keeps a group moving toward consensus. "When people are invited to come together to share their ideas, concerns, and needs they become engaged. They move from being passive recipients of instructions to committed champions of decisions. This is the power of deciding together" (Dressler, 2004, p. 2). This suggests that the very process of moving from individual commitment to consensus creates an incredible energy that can be used to implement a group's task. Likewise, completed tasks and accomplishments offer energy and encouragement to deepen the process of consensus building.

The paradox of consensus building is that it depends on group members' possessing their own well-thought-through perspectives while at the same time giving up their competitive desires to win every point of their perspective (Dressler, 2004, p. 3). Furthermore, "group members must be willing to give up 'ownership' of their ideas and allow those ideas to be refined as concerns and ideas are put on the table" (Dressler, 2004, p. 4).

Individual commitment has to do with creating the atmosphere that treats every individual as a valued human being. The challenge is fostering an atmosphere people are frankly delighted to be a part of. This is a daunting task for the manager or leader of any team or group. "Great managers look *inward*. They look inside the company, into each individual, into the differences in style, goals, needs, and motivation of each person. . . . These subtle differences guide them toward the right way to release each person's unique talents into performance" (Buckingham & Coffman, 1999, p. 63). When this kind of honoring of the individual happens, energy for the task and energy toward consensus are practically boundless. This view suggests that the leader, manager, or principal taps into motivation that is already present in people rather than instilling motivation when it is not present (Buckingham & Coffman, 1999, p. 92).

The atmosphere of commitment gives people the courage to risk consensus. An atmosphere of commitment is created as many individual commitments merge together into a whole environment. This environment that supports each person's deep commitments calls forth individual support for the whole group task. In so doing it enhances the courage to risk on behalf of the whole. It calls forth a daring that may not have been present before, a daring to move beyond what anyone individually may have been willing to venture previously. When an atmosphere of commitment is experienced, people begin to feel a sense of safety. When this happens, walls begin to crumble and barriers come down.

Earlier we stated the connection between involvement and commitment. We are now adding a third dimension: Involvement, Commitment, and Risk. When courage and risk are called for, first work on involvement and commitment. Risk and courage will naturally follow, and consensus will emerge almost without effort. Consensus can begin with some very small decisions. Celebrate those. Gradually, the scope and depth of consensus will increase to the crucial and most controversial areas.

Chapter 7

Eliciting Detailed Assignments: Simple Things to Do

INTRODUCTION TO ASSIGNMENTS

Clear-cut assignments make commitment concrete. Without clear assignments, there is no way to gauge individual commitment. Vague assignments pave the way to vague commitment, to say nothing of immense frustration because nothing seems to get done.

Because consensus is founded on concrete commitment, detailed and specific assignments are part of what indicates your group's potential for consensus. As people witness the completion of tasks, trust builds, and again the potential for genuine consensus increases.

A supportive atmosphere surrounding concrete assignments is crucial. People fear that they will be held personally accountable for the results of their particular assignments. This is where the next section, on collaborative teams, comes in. Although an individual name is put down next to each assignment, the team is ultimately responsible for its accomplishment. A successful team holds the tension between individual accountability and team support.

≈38≈

Task Volunteers

Individuals committed to a vision beyond their self-interest find they have energy not available when pursuing narrower goals, as will organizations that tap this level of commitment.

—Senge (1990)

Description

Opening up the floor for volunteers to complete various tasks communicates to the group full confidence that it can figure out how to accomplish these tasks. In other words, there are times when volunteers are more likely to get the job done than people who may be assigned against their will.

I am sure there are times when this may not be practical. Furthermore, some tasks may be uniquely suited to certain people. Team members or work colleagues often know who excels at what and suggest that a task be assigned to the people most qualified to do it.

As a rule, I suggest that if people have been participating all along in defining and laying out the steps of the projects, then they will also see which steps will realistically fit into their schedules and other time demands. My experience is that when people have a chance to participate in the full process and to get their ideas into the formation of the necessary projects, they are always willing to put themselves behind the successful completion of the projects. Volunteering for the tasks eliminates one source of excuses.

Did You Know?

- When people are involved in planning from the start, many actually want to help complete the project.
- We tend to pour extra energy into tasks we want to do.
- Task volunteering creates a snowball effect—each new step volunteered for creates a milieu that calls for more volunteering.

Activity: Task Volunteers

This activity rests on the assumption that your team wants to see the project completed. Your style here communicates absolute trust in their competence and desire to finish the project.

1. From the start, you, as the leader, need to communicate that this team is an action team. The team members have a right to know from the start that they are part of the implementation as well as the planning.

2. The team needs to be a part of both creating the big chunks of the task and breaking down the task into individual steps.

3. At this point, an appropriate question you could ask is "How shall we divide up the task to get all the steps accomplished?"

4. It may happen that one or two difficult steps are left without volunteers. In these cases perhaps two people will take responsibility for completing a task that one person was not willing to volunteer for. Or perhaps you need to ask if the responsibility can be divided into even smaller chunks.

5. Once these steps are passed out, your only concern as a general rule is the *completion* of the task, not the *method* of completing the task. This focus demonstrates your trust in the group.

6. It is crucial to set the next meeting time and to clarify exactly what is expected to be accomplished by that meeting.

Hints

- If there is reluctance to volunteer, then as much as possible let the rest of the members push each other to volunteer. Team members will be more receptive to their peers' pushing them than to a traditional top-down assignment.
- At the end of the volunteering session, you might ask, "Does all this seem realistic?" If there are concerns, let the group handle them.
- Ideally, the leader has enough rapport with the group that spot checking between meetings will be seen as a method of support. If there are implementation problems, the question from the leader is, "How can the team help you?" or "How can I help you?" rather than "Why haven't you been able to get this done?"

Example

A group entered a planning workshop very disgruntled over its work situation. A number of issues and complaints were aired during the planning. After an excellent planning workshop, it came time to divide into teams. Would one person make the assignments? Would we take volunteers (the preferable method)?

The group suggested putting everyone's name in a hat and drawing names one at a time to fill each team. Those randomly selected teams have been highly functional ever since. The group decided that this process of creating teams would demonstrate its own commitment to starting out in a radically new way, breaking with any tendency to operate by cliques or friendships. The decision symbolized an amazing depth of individual commitment and trust.

⨾39⨾

What/Who/When Cards

*As we make and keep commitments . . . we begin to estab-
lish an inner integrity that gives us the awareness of self-
control and the courage and strength to accept more of the
responsibility for our own lives.*

—Covey (1990)

Description

Cards can be used to record the individual steps needed to
carry out an assignment. The step, the name of the person
who is going to do it, and the completion date can all be written on one card.

These same cards can be used in conjunction with Activity 40,
Timelines. They can be put onto a timeline and then moved
around as necessary. These cards are another way to keep before
everyone's eyes the tasks of each individual and the commitments individuals are making toward accomplishing their task.

Did You Know?

- Many people need help imagining all the little steps
  involved in completing a project.
- What may seem like time-consuming specificity on the
  front end saves a great deal of time down the line.

- What/Who/When cards leave little room for wondering how something is going to get done.

Activity: What/Who/When Cards

1. Prepare the blank What/Who/When cards ahead of time.

2. Pass out the cards to each group.

3. For each project, have everyone brainstorm the ten to fifteen steps it will take to accomplish the project.

4. Write the steps on the cards, one step per card.

5. Have the teams fill out the "who" and "when" categories. Have individuals volunteer for the tasks to be done and then write their names on the cards.

6. Have the teams lay their cards out on the table or the wall, which may help clarify the flow or provide additional insights into effective implementation.

Hints

- Very often I have groups that initially write only one or two cards to carry out a project. In those cases I ask questions such as the following: "When will you decide where the meeting is going to be?" "How are you going to let people know about the meeting?" "Where is the meeting going to be?" "Are there going to be refreshments?" "Who is going to clean up?" Suddenly people realize the myriad steps it takes to implement any project successfully.

- Completing these cards helps the group see what lies ahead. Again, ask the question of realism frequently. If one person has too much to accomplish, figure that out ahead of time if possible and suggest shifting some assignments around to make the responsibilities more realistic.

Example

This card illustrates one step of many in planning a commemorative dinner.

WHAT	
Contact main speaker	
WHO	WHEN
Jack	By March 3

❦40❦

Timelines

The Implementation Timeline . . . will serve as the check-point for future review sessions.

—Spencer (1989)

Description

A visual timeline can be an extremely valuable tool in laying out the tasks ahead. I suggest doing a timeline for several months or a year to give people an accurate understanding of the big picture. Then move to a smaller time period to allow the kind of detail people need to make realistic judgments about the feasibility and realism of what they want to accomplish.

It is easy for people to make promises in a vacuum: "Of course I can do these three steps." Those three steps may be relatively simple. But what about the fifty other tasks that have not been included on the timeline? A comprehensive and complete timeline, not just for one team but for all the teams in a group, will help everyone see the whole picture and may even avoid conflicts.

Did You Know?

- Graphic timelines can reveal time conflicts early enough to change your plans.

- Time openings revealed on a graphic timeline allow you to use that time wisely instead of cramming things into a later, more crowded time block.
- Graphic timelines are a guideline or a support, not a rule book or a whip being cracked over you.

Activity: Timelines

1. Using 5 × 8 cards, lay out the major projects or tasks down the left side of a wall and the months or weeks across the top.

2. Have the team write out the steps for each task and place them under the appropriate week or month column. See Activity 39, What/Who/When Cards.

3. When the entire picture is up on the wall, ask the team, "What do you notice?" or "What is this timeline revealing to us?"

4. If too many of the team's steps or accomplishments occur in the same week, the group can make alterations. The timeline may also reveal that several teams have chosen the same week for a major effort, and this scheduling also may need to be changed.

5. Ask, "What changes would make this timeline more realistic?"

6. You might also ask, "Now that you see the whole picture, what duplicate steps do you see across the teams?" or "What steps could be combined?"

7. It is very tempting to make helpful suggestions yourself, but asking questions instead puts the responsibility for decisions back on the team.

Hints

- Understanding not just the flow of each project but the flow of each project in relationship to every other project is crucial here. The visual aspect of the timeline can be extremely helpful.

- Once the entire timeline has been reviewed and polished, I ask the group to step back and imagine it has reached the end of the timeline and almost everything has been accomplished. Then I ask, "What new position will we be in if all this gets done?" This question helps people gain a stance of victory, which can sustain them through the accomplishment of the projects.

Example

TIMELINE					
	AUG.	SEPT.	OCT.	NOV.	DEC.
PROJECT ONE	□□□ □□	□ □ □	□	□	
PROJECT TWO	□ □	□ □	□□□ □ □	□ □	□
PROJECT THREE	□ □	□ □ □	□	□ □ □ □	□
PROJECT FOUR	□	□	□ □ □	□ □	□□□ □ □

❧41❧

Attendance

Consensus implies commitment to a decision. When group members commit to a decision they oblige themselves to do their part in putting that decision into action.

—Dressler (2004)

Description

This activity suggests the importance of acknowledging who is around the table and who is not. I am not suggesting that every person's name be read, but rather that particular mention can be made of all who are not present and why they are not present.

This is a simple way to dramatize that every single individual on the team is important to the task (and to consensus). We may be tempted to gloss over people's absences, but to do so communicates that those people are not important—or that ultimately individuals are not important to the whole team. Everyone on the team deserves to know where the absent people are. This honors those who have been able to carry out their commitment to be present.

Did You Know?

- Each human being who makes it to your meeting is crucial to the success of the whole task.

- People are willing to work hard in a meeting when they understand clearly why others are not able to make the meeting.
- People need reminders that even though one or two may be absent, it is still possible to get the necessary work accomplished.

Activity: Attendance

In one way this activity is simple. The absence of people can subtly drain the group. Unless we say otherwise, absence can communicate that the absent person is not committed to the team.

1. For example, say, "As you know, John is out sick today, and Sally is at the district office in a meeting with the manager. Both of them said they would call me tomorrow and get filled in on our meeting today."

2. Continue by saying, "We are not all here, but I believe the rest of us can carry out what we need to do today" or "It is hard when we are not all here, but let's see how as one team we can get our tasks done today."

Hints

- How we handle absences sets the tone of a meeting. By taking absences too lightly, we subtly devalue a team member; for example, "John never says much when he is here anyway" or "It's OK; we do not really need Sally today."
- Another temptation is to use an absence as an excuse for venting frustration or anger: "How can we get our work done if all these people do not show up?" or "What is the matter, don't John and Sally realize how much work we have to finish?" Such statements communicate a lot about our views of John and Sally.
- Many people feel that any effort in this direction treats the team and its members as little children, as if

acknowledging who is there and who is not somehow demeans people. To the contrary, I suggest keeping attendance is a powerful tool, when done well, in honoring the individuals who are expending their commitment and energy on the tasks at hand.

Example

Many times when a facilitator leads a meeting of thirty or forty people, one or two will come up and explain that they have to leave early for a particular commitment. Facilitators make sure each person who takes the time to talk to them knows how much it is appreciated. Facilitators explain what will be covered so those leaving early will know what to ask their team members about when they return. Frequently, facilitators give the departing member an additional assignment. Facilitators ought to scrupulously avoid saying things like "Oh, well, there are so many people here, I would not have noticed anyway" or "Didn't you know when you signed up that you had to be here the full time?"

It is time to communicate to people that we know they are intelligent, important people who live in a swirl of overwhelming responsibilities. The situation can be very different, however, if you know beforehand that you are dealing with someone who is shirking responsibility. In this case, the facilitator would offer this person two alternatives, both of which are acceptable, each of which would demonstrate picking up more responsibility. For example, the alternatives could be reading an article and sharing it with the group or writing a short paragraph laying out a plan for a new project or a new approach in teaching.

∽42∽

Assignment Chart

Transformational leaders do not fall into the trap of treating people as cogs in the mechanism. They treat people as individuals who are seeking their own satisfaction and fulfillment.

—Ritscher (in Adams, 1986)

Description

This activity suggests that assignments be written out or typed up and made available in a chart for all to have. The names of each person on the team need to be listed. The particular tasks and steps and the names of those who will be doing them are written out or typed up and passed out or posted for everyone to see.

A printed chart informs everyone of what fellow team members are doing. This is a way of supporting everyone's commitment. People often put forth a little extra effort when they know that everyone else knows they have agreed and are responsible for a task or project. In addition, people often put forth extra effort because of how much effort everyone else is putting forth.

Did You Know?

- People are empowered when they have a clear idea what everyone else is working on.

- People are reminded of the whole task when they see the full picture represented in a comprehensive assignment chart.
- The assignment chart objectively communicates to each person that everyone is depending on each particular task in order for the whole project to get done.

Activity: Assignment Chart

1. As teams are laying out their implementation steps or as they are filling out their What/Who/When cards (Activity 39), have them fill in an assignment chart.

2. After the teams have reported and adjustments have been made, collect these charts and have them typed up.

3. Make sure that everyone gets a copy of these charts.

PROJECT: *New Marketing Brochure*		
STEPS	WHO	WHEN
1. Finalize product name	John	April 3
2. Write descriptive paragraphs	Beth	April 10
3. Get info to layout person	Dan	April 12
4. Get first draft back from layout person	Dan	April 15
5. Revise the final draft	Beth	April 17
6. Draft back to layout person	Dan	April 19
7. Pick up revised brochure	Dan	April 23
8. Get approval from manager	John	April 24
9. Send to printer	Vicki	April 25
10. Pick up brochures from printer	Vicki	May 1
11. Send to mail house for mailing	Vicki	May 2
12. Check to see if brochure has been received	Dan	May 10

Hints

- An assignment chart is a tool to enhance individual commitment as well as to help the group remember who is to do what.
- Making sure that everyone has a copy is a great way to dramatize the commitments many have made to getting things done. It is even more impressive if the assignments have been made by the team and not by one person in a top-down way. This clearly shows the involvement of every individual on the team.
- Individual commitments can be enhanced when this tool is used to strengthen and support the team. Avoid using this as a tool to beat people over the head with a task or project not yet completed; doing so will make people unwilling to link their names with specific tasks.

Example

Before working for a company, a facilitator was given a three-ring binder with every team's plans. A copy of this binder went to everyone. When it came time to report, each person could see how much of the plan had been accomplished. The plans were very specific, and many included graphs and charts that clarified the progress the teams intended to make throughout the implementation of their plans.

Crucial to having the reporting come off in the celebrative way it did was the nonjudgmental attitude that permeated the room. If things had not gone according to plan, people were asked the reason and how their future plans could benefit from the work of the previous time period. This atmosphere went a long way to deepening individual commitment.

Chapter 8

Expanding Personal Recognition: Things That Take Effort

INTRODUCTION TO RECOGNITION

Recognition is a *lateral* form of honoring the people working on your team. In the past, honor always went to people hierarchically higher than you, to people older than you, or it went downward in the form of reward and recognition from higher-ups. In this age of all people coming to a new sense of their own self-worth, motivation to work together increases as people sense their contributions are understood and valued by those with whom they are working side by side.

In other words, an environment that recognizes and appreciates each person's individual gifts fosters and nurtures individual commitment. We expect more and more responsibility from individuals today. People can actually increase their commitment as personal recognition is expanded.

Consensus is difficult if not impossible to achieve in an atmosphere of distrust and an environment that denigrates individuals. In such an atmosphere, personal survival quickly becomes the goal. Rapidly a milieu grows in which the norm is to do only the very minimum required. Deep consensus will more likely emerge if people experience recognition of their gifts, for in such an atmosphere people will increasingly want the team, with its plans and projects, to win.

❦43❧

Specific Praise

Unprecedented information-sharing, interaction, and recognition are required to induce the attitude change and horizontal communication necessary to foster wide-spread involvement and commitment.

—Peters (1987)

Description

Praise is often difficult to offer. There are mindsets that say, "Why praise people for just doing their jobs?" or "Work is its own reward, so praise does not need to be offered" or "If I praise, then people will relax and not work." All these mindsets create an atmosphere that is stingy on praise.

Other people find it easy to praise. They are always saying, "That's a great job" or "You are the best secretary I have ever had." This kind of praise may make both the giver and the receiver feel good for a moment, but it is not very helpful.

Specific praise pinpoints the precise action or accomplishment that merits praise and names it to the individual. This fosters a genuineness and believability in the interaction. Specific praise helps people know exactly the kind of action, activity, or accomplishment to perform again. People have a right, more than once a year during a performance appraisal, to learn where they stand.

Did You Know?

- A minute of praise and recognition can result in an hour of extra energy toward the task.
- Even if praise and recognition sound phony at first, gradually they become more genuine.
- Praise and appreciation are contagious; they can spread not only through the company but even to the clients.

Activity: Specific Praise

Because this type of recognition is not natural for most of us right away, you may need to practice ahead of time.

1. There are several models, but one I find helpful is from Robert Bolton's book *People Skills* (1979, p. 183):

   When you . . . I feel . . . because . . .

2. When you first try this, you may want to write it out ahead of time to clarify to yourself what you want to say.

3. It might look like the following:
   a. "When you finished that report two days early, I was delighted because that allowed the department heads to read and approve it before I had to send it on to the Regional Manager."
   b. "When you led the meeting so smoothly, I was delighted because people left feeling they knew the important information and were ready to make a decision on the matter next week."
   c. "When you took the extra time to meet with that upset client, I was pleased because that demonstrated that we care about customer service."

Hints

- Some people are so unaccustomed to hearing such direct communication that it might be necessary to repeat the praise once or twice until you get a clue that your point has been clearly heard and understood.

- This same pattern can be used to communicate to an employee or fellow worker something that needs to be corrected.
- Some workplaces establish an "employee-of-the-month" program, complete with a luncheon with the boss and perhaps other recognition tokens. If such a program is used, make sure that the specifics of the employee's performance are highlighted so that everyone understands the kinds of concrete actions that are being celebrated and rewarded in your particular job environment.

Example

The following represents how one group figured out how to give specific praise. Your team will need to experiment with what is appropriate and works for it. Every three months, an educational training and publishing company passed out three kinds of awards to its employees: Special Contribution—for contributions beyond the call of duty; Team Building—for efforts that enable a team or teams; and Peak Performance—for contributions that illustrate individual effort for the good of the company. Each award specifically mentioned the particular activity or accomplishment that merited the award. At the end of the year, the number and kind of awards received determined the number of tickets that each employee earned toward a drawing for the yearly company employee prize. Just receiving the awards throughout the year increased good feelings about work. The prize at the end of the year was something concrete that symbolized the company's commitment to the employees. As you walked through the office, you saw that many employees had posted their awards by their desks.

∽44∾

Individual Celebrations

Celebrations have a powerful contribution to make.

—Owen (1987)

Description

Individual celebrations—those related either to personal life or to work and professional life—are critical to acknowledge. Many teams are already good at noting people's birthdays, a degree received, or a promotion earned. In addition, a specific victory with a challenging project, a leading role in pulling off a major event, or an article written for a magazine can be causes for celebration.

In our work-permeated life, I once heard someone say that we just cannot have too many celebrations. When something out of the ordinary happens, even five minutes of celebration can lift everyone's spirits for the next twenty-four hours.

Did You Know?

- An appropriate celebration for an individual's accomplishment or birthday is an opportunity to show appreciation for that person's unique gifts.
- Individual celebrations are opportunities for all members of the group to step back and think about their own life journey.

- Small, appropriate celebrations that feed people's connections to each other not only add building blocks for consensus but add motivation for accomplishing the tasks as well.

Activity: Individual Celebrations

1. Customarily, we think of food and drink when it comes time for celebration. These things do wonders.

2. In addition, a key question or two in the midst of noting someone's individual celebration can cause everyone to stand back and reflect a moment:
   a. What does it mean to you now that you have your master's degree?
   b. What has been the most significant event for you in this last year?
   c. What are you looking forward to in the year to come?
   d. What do you feel has been one of your key accomplishments in your role as department head?
   e. What did you discover as you wrote that article?
   f. What did you learn about teams as your team successfully completed that difficult task?
   g. What kept you going?

3. Five or ten minutes at the beginning or end of a meeting can be used from time to time for celebrating. For some it seems like time wasted. For the wise facilitator, it is the stuff that keeps individuals motivated and energized.

Hints

- Key questions that cause people to think and reflect can begin to call forth responses about what gives meaning and worth to them in the midst of often-hectic lives. People are eager to hear their colleagues speak about these things.

- Although something like this at every team meeting may seem impractical, something like this every month is not too often.
- This activity calls for you as the facilitator to be alert to the informal conversations going on as people gather or during break times so that opportunities for authentic individual celebrations can be capitalized on when they occur.

Example

A team member had immigrated to the United States from another country and received his doctorate after a great deal of study in this country. The team decided to hold a small celebration. At that time, they asked him what this degree meant to him. After acknowledging that the work had been hard, especially working in English as his second language, he commented, "Because of the upheaval in my country, I can never return there. I have no other place to go. I am grateful for this place to work." That is the kind of reflective comment that can push the thinking of everyone listening. Many in the group started to wonder if they could endure experiences like their team member had and still be as gracious and affirming of life as he was. Would they have had the stamina to work as hard as he had? His comment called forth deep appreciation for the spirit of such a human being. As said earlier, it may take only five or ten minutes, but a lot can happen to people when such opportunities occur.

≈45≈

Training, Coaching, or Project Feedback

There is nothing more important to an individual committed to his or her own growth than a supportive environment.

—Senge (1990)

Description

Occasionally you are called on to give feedback after a training session, a presentation, or a project. These are times of great anxiety for both the individual who is waiting for feedback and the people who are called on to give feedback.

The key is understanding that the task is enabling the individual to do his or her own reflection on his or her own presentation or project. This runs counter to the temptation to tell the person everything done well and everything not done so well. An environment that seeks to strengthen individuals seeks to deepen their own capacity to reflect on their performance.

Consequently, the coach's role, rather than giving specific feedback, is to create, through specific questions, an occasion for processing and reflection. In addition to that, objective data may be shared when the individual asks such questions as "What questions did I actually ask?" or "How much time did I really take in this section?" or "During my presentation, what percentage of my time did I spend actually looking at the audience?"

Did You Know?

- The most important outcome of this activity is not perfect performance but growing trust.
- When this activity is done well, people want to do it again.
- Listening well can help you grasp what crucial question to ask.

Activity: Training, Coaching, or Project Feedback

Do this activity after a person has demonstrated a new skill, made a presentation, or completed a project. This activity is a conversation with the person who has just done one of these things. The presupposition in this whole set of questions is that insights that occur to people on their own mean more than someone else's "good ideas." Here are four basic questions to ask.

1. *What was your plan?* or *What did you intend to do?* Even if this was talked about earlier, it is helpful to start at this safe point. Occasionally the original plan may have changed at the last moment because of new information. Consequently, hearing exactly what was intended can clarify things not understood in the presentation.

2. *What do you sense came off well?* or *What do you think worked well?* or *What parts were of particularly high quality?* Again, please avoid the huge temptation to give your direct feedback. Your job is to foster the person's own critical thinking.

3. *When you do this again, what might you do differently?* This immediately enables the person to engage in a thoughtful review and encourages some self-reflection on ways to improve.

4. *How can I help?* or *In what ways can we assist you?* This continues to put the person in total control of the continuation of the coaching process.

Hints

- This activity assumes it is possible for people to increase and deepen their capacity to assess their own performance. Furthermore, it suggests that another person can assist in this growth just by asking questions.
- It may be helpful to take notes yourself during the presentation or report so that you have clear and objective information to share.
- Amazingly, when this is done in a style of encouragement and specificity, people grow in confidence and in appreciation for the opportunity to do their own thinking.

Example

A trainer led a two-day workshop for administrators, the focus of which was training in a structured method to carry out a participatory workshop. After experiencing the method and reviewing the steps and theory behind it, the group divided into teams to prepare to lead a portion of the workshop the next day in a role-play situation.

After each of the administrators led a section of the full workshop, the trainer paused to ask them what they had done well. Responses included the following: "I was nervous at first but gradually became more confident," "My team prepared me well ahead of time," and "I had everything written down in front of me so I didn't get confused." The trainer then asked the members what they might do differently next time. People offered comments such as the following: "Next time I will practice first in front of a mirror," "I would look people more directly in the eyes," and "I would ask someone else to write on the chart paper because it is hard for me to write and concentrate at the same time." The encouraging style of the group and the nature of the questions created a nonthreatening atmosphere that fostered self-assessment.

≈46≈

Use of People's Names

There is a widely held myth that "Personal is personal, and work is work, and never the twain shall meet." But in actuality, "personal" and "work" are always integrally combined.

—Ritscher (in Adams, 1986)

Description

Whenever possible during my facilitation, I try to use people's names in responding to them. The mood of the group shifts when names are used during the interaction. The group begins to congeal.

A name is one of the most personal aspects of an individual. Just as people respond almost immediately if they are called by the wrong name or if their name is misspelled or mispronounced, they also respond positively inside when they are addressed correctly. Getting their names right is another way of acknowledging that you are working with unique individuals.

Did You Know?

- Hearing people's names creates an atmosphere of connection.
- People open up a little when their name is used.

- Our high-tech, high-touch environment has created a need for more appropriate informality rather than for stiffer formality.

Activity: Use of People's Names

This activity suggests you find ways such as name tags or name cards to make names available when you don't know them already.

1. Although it may seem easier to use this technique with a small group you have been meeting with for a long time, it still requires discipline to mention names in the course of dialogue.

    "So, Tom, what you are saying is that the project you are recommending would benefit not only the clients but the company, too."

    "Mary, tell us a little more about what is involved with that."

2. Sometimes, a person speaks up in strong opposition to what most of the group has been saying. Instead of passing over the comment in an attempt to move on, I use such a comment as an opportunity to remind people that any group has many perspectives.

    "Note that from Stan's perspective, although this program would definitely increase revenue, the average cost per item does not warrant the expense. Let's hear another perspective."

    "What Joan said reminds us that when we suggested something like this last year, several other staff people voiced strong objections about it to the manager."

    "Steve is concerned that the employees are going to have a hard time buying into this."

3. If I am working with a new group, during the introductory conversation, I make a little drawing of the table and fill in people's names as I hear them. This gives me another tool to refer to when I want to use a person's name.

Hints

- One reason I repeat an opposing position with the person's name is to make sure the group hears the comment and also to make sure the individual knows that we have heard the comment. Then if a different decision is finally reached, the individual knows without a doubt that the opposing perspective was at least heard in the process of coming to another resolution of the issue.
- If this is your first time in front of a large group, name tags can be extremely helpful. As a person is speaking, I will glance at the name tag so that I can respond to the comment with the correct name.
- If the group is large, of course you will not be able to remember everyone's name. However, even if you use the names of only twenty percent of the group, you move the group much closer to a feeling of familiarity and closeness and personal recognition. Even if you use only the names of the people who talk most frequently, the dynamic of using personal names has been established and is working in the group's favor.

Example

Occasionally people come to a facilitator and say, "How do you remember everyone's name?" The truth is that most of the time the facilitator has not remembered them at all but has used their name tags or a seating chart or has used the names of only ten people out of the forty in the group. But the fact that the comment is made communicates that the facilitator's use of people's names has been noticed and has helped people feel recognized.

⇒47⇐

Personalized Job Tools

Work is more than what you do to earn a paycheck; it involves personal commitment, personal satisfaction, and personal growth.

—Ritscher (in Adams, 1986)

Description

From time to time, or during a holiday, the facilitator may want to show concrete recognition of the team. Circumstances vary, of course, but one way this can be done is to give something that enhances people's sense of job professionalism.

Sometimes employees have a low image of their job or role, which can have a huge impact on employee morale. Consequently, personalized job tools that enhance a sense of professionalism have the possibility of increasing workers' self-image. Genuine experiences of self-worth increase individual commitment. A personalized job tool can help employees perform their job better, and it may also have their name on it.

Did You Know?

- Every time employees use such a job tool, they are reminded of their connections to their work colleagues.
- An appropriate job tool can communicate "I believe you are a professional just as I am."

- A personalized job tool can help re-create a person's self-image.

Activity: Personalized Job Tools

1. What you do in this area depends greatly on your own analysis of the group with which you are working. What you do also needs to fit your own personality. Ask yourself these questions:
   a. What is the mood of this group? How are people feeling about themselves? Has a particular project been giving the group members a rough time?
   b. How are they feeling about what is going to happen next in their work?
   c. Is a recognition of the whole team needed more than individual recognition at the moment?
   d. What job tool can I offer that will encourage the individuals?

2. Answering some of these questions may help you discern what kind of concrete recognition would be most helpful for your group.

3. Possible personalized job tools include the following:
   a. Name plates for the desk
   b. Appointment books
   c. Note pads: "From Jim's desk . . ."
   d. Wall calendars
   e. Attractive pictures for wall space

Hints

- I notice that many recognition items I hear about do not cost a lot of money. Yet the impact is inestimable.
- Even an idea that seems a little corny may be just the thing to perk up a group's spirit when it is lagging or overburdened.

Example

Recently a principal in New York state decided that as a holiday gift, he would give each staff member a personalized set of business cards. Many had never had their own business cards before. Whether or not all the staff used their cards, the gift communicated to them that the principal felt they were professionals.

As part of an ongoing program of employee recognition, one company named an employee of the month and granted that person a parking space near the front entrance for the month. This costs absolutely no money but goes a long way toward building morale.

Chapter 9

Occasioning Individual Accountability and Absolution: For the Committed

INTRODUCTION TO ACCOUNTABILITY AND ABSOLUTION

How do you enable people to sustain their motivation and commitment to work? In the past, the primary method involved threats and fear: "If you do not do A, B will happen." "You do it this way or you will lose your job or not get a raise." Such an environment encourages hiding the truth. In other words, if things are not going so well, employees dare not reveal that there is any problem at all. In such an atmosphere, they present only the most glowingly positive facts and attempt to keep any other facts hidden from view.

In the supportive team environment, it is possible to share the truth. An uncompleted project, a failed experiment, a risk that has fallen flat on its face, a forgotten task—all these, as well as successes and victories, can be acknowledged. The team knows it can proceed successfully only if the real situation is fully known. Once the facts are out on the table, the team can use its power to figure out the next move and to create the support that enables the entire team to move forward. The team does this by demanding honesty and truth in its reporting and by pronouncing absolution on the situation as it is. This chapter falls in the Individual Commitment section because fear and threats reduce commitment whereas honesty and absolution increase commitment by enabling the entire team to move forward. This environment inspires individual commitment and freely given energy for the task.

By further cementing the individuals to the team, this approach enhances the environment for consensus. This atmosphere energizes the team to *want* to find points of agreement. As team interdependence and individual commitment grow, so does the foundation for deeper consensus.

≈48≈

Short Weekly Meetings

By making and keeping promises to ourselves and others, little by little, our honor becomes greater than our moods.

—Covey (1990)

Description

Regular and short check-in meetings to discuss honestly what is happening are crucial to carrying out projects smoothly. Getting the true picture out on the table provides a way to focus team energy, not only on planning the next phase but also on resolving particular issues or stumbling blocks.

When these meetings happen crisply and regularly, they deepen the team connection and therefore continue to enhance the possibility of more and more consensus across the team.

Did You Know?

- Many times we shy away from meeting with our colleagues because we fear we have not done enough.
- Short, consistent, regular meetings are part of a weekly rhythm people can begin to anticipate positively.
- Short weekly meetings can be regarded as supports to getting work done rather than as undesired interruptions of work flow.

Activity: Short Weekly Meetings

1. You might begin by reminding the team of the larger task of which it is a part or by mentioning the teams performing other parts of the task.

2. Next, each team member can honestly report about what has been accomplished in the previous week and what is left to be done.

3. Following all the reports, I suggest the insertion of some word of affirmation. A sentence that announces to the whole team the completion of the previous time period and acknowledges all the accomplishments, as well as omissions or errors, provides the environment to move the team unencumbered into the future. This kind of statement or affirmation is what is being referred to as absolution. It is a way of saying that whatever has happened has been acknowledged and that now it is time to move on. Note that it occurs after the full picture of the situation has been shared.

4. At this moment it is possible for the team to look at the next time period and perhaps make adjustments in tasks, in who is to do which task, and so on.

5. You can conclude with brief announcements as well as a word on when the next meeting is. You may choose to end with some sentence or phrase that reminds people of the deeper effort to which all are committed.

Hints

- Step 3 may feel very awkward for a while. I can assure you that as it becomes more familiar and genuine, you pave the way for team members to be more truthful. Furthermore, as stated earlier, you are beckoning forth deeper individual commitment.
- When a task is not done, leaders often experience a strong temptation to ask immediately, "Why didn't you get this

done?" or "What is the matter with you?" Sometimes it is helpful to ask the person to say more about what has been going on so that you and the team get more information. An accusatory question provokes defensiveness and may lead the person being accused to blame someone else or withhold information. A request for more background information can lead you closer to the real issue.

- Accountability and absolution assume a team of responsible individuals.

Example

LIST OF ABSOLUTIONS

1. The past week is over, and we are free to create the week to come.

2. This week has been difficult and trying. It is also finished. This week's victories and accomplishments beckon us forward.

3. Both our successes and our failures are now part of the past. We are totally free to create the future.

4. We can release both our successes and our failures and now proceed unburdened to create the week to come.

5. This week, complete with its successes and struggles, now can inform us about how to do the tasks ahead.

6. (Go ahead, write your own absolution.)

_____

_____

For many years, a friend belonged to an organization that demanded long hours and lots of energy for the tasks the members had decided to accomplish. They met weekly, frequently repeating sentences like the examples above. The fact that they kept on doing this work year after year is directly related to their constantly invoking statements like those.

⁓49⁓

"I Am Nervous About" Conversations

With increasing turbulence, transience, and complexity in our society, both organizational and individual excellence will be at a premium.

—Adams (1984)

Description

Some duties, tasks, or responsibilities occasion a lot of anxiety. It is possible to bring that anxiety into the open and lessen the control it has on people's behavior. This activity breaks the vicious cycle of accusing, blaming, and denying by affirming that although many parts of our work are pleasing to us, each of us is also required to do tasks that annoy us or make us nervous.

Did You Know?

- More people are anxious and nervous than we can imagine.
- Many times being anxious and nervous can reveal that people care about a task or project.
- There are some tasks about which it is very wise to be anxious.

Activity: "I Am Nervous About" Conversations

1. Divide the group into pairs.
2. Ask each pair to discuss the following questions:

    a. What are you looking forward to in the implementation of this task?

    b. What are you fearful of, nervous about, or afraid of as you think of yourself carrying out this task?

    c. What are some strategies each of you has found helpful in carrying out tasks that cause a lot of anxiety?

    d. Some people use 3 × 5 cards to write themselves messages of encouragement. What message would you put on a 3 × 5 card to encourage yourself during this task?

3. Now that everyone has been through this conversation in pairs, you might ask each question of the total group and request that some share the answers they talked about in pairs.

4. If you do not have time for the whole-group discussion, you could ask a general question, such as "What did you talk about?" "What surprised you in your conversations?" or "What did you learn during your conversations?"

Hints

- With a particularly astute group, you might even ask a deeper question, such as "Why did I decide to hold this conversation with you?"

- At every point, you are trying to communicate that nervousness, anxiety, and tiredness are naturally a part of many tasks and activities. By talking about these feelings openly, we indirectly free ourselves from them, thereby liberating ourselves to participate more calmly in the tasks at hand.

- The intent of this conversation is to increase individual involvement and commitment so that greater team cohesiveness will result in deeper levels of consensus and energy for the task.

Example

After a group had been trained in the kind of workshop methods that have been talked about in this book, the time approached to use the methods to lead community focus groups. It was clear that anxieties were running very high.

After the members formed pairs, the leader asked a series of questions similar to the ones in this activity. Afterward the whole group was asked to volunteer some of the responses they had shared in pairs.

People seemed to be comforted by hearing many others express similar anxieties. Because of their heightened level of comfort, they could pay better attention to those courageous individuals who could express hope and confidence in the midst of their anxieties.

≈50≈

Implementation Lesson Conversation

The ultimate stage of involvement is the regular, sponta-neous taking of initiative.

—Peters (1987)

Description

A very indirect way of attaining accountability and abso-lution is through a structured conversation that recognizes not only people's accomplishments and struggles but also the lessons people have learned while carrying out their tasks.

This activity creates a new context for the efforts of the past time period. Usually people can recall only how tough it has been or the failures they have had. Pulling out of an experi-ence some gems of learning and insight can wrap the difficult experience in a new light, which can free the group to move into the next time period with hope and confidence.

Did You Know?

- Even disasters have hidden lessons.
- People grow more proficient when you take a moment to talk about what they have learned.
- Many lessons do not reveal themselves until called forth in the midst of intentional conversation.

Activity: Implementation Lesson Conversation

This conversation is best had at the conclusion of a natural time period or at the completion of a project. It is most effective when everyone on the team is present. Proceed from one question to the next when the group has provided four or five responses.

1. In the past quarter, what have been some of our key accomplishments and victories?

2. What are some things that worked well for us?

3. What were some of our hardest struggles?

4. What were some failures?

5. How are we in a different position than we were three months ago?

6. What are some things we have learned through the activities we have implemented in these past three months?

7. What changes can we suggest now for how we go about things in the next three months?

8. What title shall we give these past three months? (e.g., "The Great Quarter of _____ .")

Hints

- The value of a conversation such as this is that it is carried out totally from a team perspective. No one person's accomplishments or failures are highlighted. This perspective provides one form of accountability and absolution.
- The assumption of this conversation is that even our failures teach us something valuable and can assist us in the future.

- This conversation in no way suggests that there are no longer any differences. When differences arise, the individually committed team members want to work hard at finding a solution that will work and satisfy the perspectives and values represented.
- A slight modification of this conversation could be used to help an individual get perspective on something that did not turn out well. The flow of these questions can also be used to help people step back and process a disaster.
- This is not, of course, a weekly conversation. However, it could easily be a regular quarterly one.

Example

From leading this entire conversation with several teams, I have collected the following lessons shared by team members:

1. Successful implementation increases team and individual confidence.

2. Successful implementation sparks other successes.

3. A well-chosen project can transform the mood of an entire organization.

4. Success invites others on board.

5. Finding ways to keep regularly connected with the other teams is crucial.

6. We need some work as a whole group to map out how we intend to make decisions together.

～51～

A Victory Party Before the Victory

Involvement can start with anything. Maybe even a party.

—Peters (1987)

Description

It is not uncommon to hold a victory celebration after a task is completed. This activity, however, suggests holding a victory celebration *before* the event. In other words, use such an event to project everyone into a winning spirit before the victory occurs. You are proclaiming with confidence that there is no way your team can lose. This is a bold claim. It acknowledges ahead of time that not everything will go perfectly. It also declares ahead of time that the plan has been created with victory built into it. It proclaims that no matter what mistakes may occur in implementation, the plan is failureproof.

This is a radical declaration of absolution that takes everyone's fears and worries and places them in a context of victory.

Did You Know?

- A victory party before the victory communicates that the group will experience a victory whether it occurs or not.
- Everyone wants to be part of a winning team; the wise leader helps everyone see they are winners already.

Activity: A Victory Party Before the Victory

This activity suggests doing something confident and maybe a little outrageous before your task is completed: declaring your victory before you have won.

1. As the leader, pay attention to the mood of your group.

2. If anxieties are running high about a particularly critical project or event, ask, "What could we do to celebrate ahead of time our confidence that we are going to win at this?"

3. On chart paper, make a list of the suggestions from the group. Some possibilities could be going out to dinner, going to a movie, or having refreshments at the next meeting.

4. Talk for a minute about the values of each possibility and what each one communicates.

5. Choose one and set a time.

6. Quickly divide up the responsibilities.

Hints

- The key is to let the group put the particulars together.
- The very idea of a victory celebration before the victory may seem very offensive to hard-liner types. This kind of event cannot be forced.
- Let the group members declare the meaning of the event. Once you have raised the idea, let them decide the significance of doing it. Such meaning cannot be preached to the group.

Example

A dozen facilitators were about to begin two full weeks of leading workshops they had never led before. Furthermore, a lot was riding on the success of these two weeks. The night before the workshops began, all the newly trained facilitators, their bosses, and the trainers gathered for a victory celebration.

They used a few moments during the party to state in a group conversation exactly what victories they were hoping for. They also spent time imagining the new position the organization would be in if all worked out well.

Needless to say, on the last day they went out to dinner to hold a "victory after the fact" celebration.

⇜52⇝

Symbol of Commitment

It could be argued that a "critical mass" of individual members need to undergo personal transformations before their organizations can undergo system-wide transformation.

—Adams (1984)

Description

Some groups have found ways to create symbols of their individual commitments to the task and to their team. This is another activity that best comes from the spontaneous decisions of the team. When it does happen, it can be very powerful in crystallizing a group's decision to work together. These symbols—which can be as simple as a team notebook for each person, with a visual symbol or a significant sentence on the inside of the notebook—can also be concrete reminders to members of their decision to work together as a team to accomplish their goal.

Did You Know?

- Participating in an appropriate symbol of commitment can be a deeply binding rite of passage.
- An appropriate symbol for one group of people may not mean anything to a different group; in other words, genuine symbols are very group specific.
- A wise leader stays alert for appropriate symbols.

Activity: Symbol of Commitment

After a group has been meeting for a while or has just experienced a real change in how it is organized or a dramatic shift in some of its responsibilities, sometimes it decides to create some kind of symbol of its intention to carry a project through to the end.

The following conversation might help the group formalize its commitment.

1. What are some of the changes we have been experiencing lately?

2. How are these changes affecting us as a group?

3. How would you talk about the way our commitment to our task is deepening?

4. What object or symbol could we create to remind us of our commitment?

Hints

- The power of this activity is in its spontaneity.
- The leader's skill lies in noticing when these symbols have emerged in the life of the team.
- Even humorous symbols can represent serious commitment.

Example

A staff had been experiencing a great deal of backbiting and gossip. After an intensive two days of creating plans for the next phase of organizational growth, the team responsible for effective leadership stood up and declared that the following week, each person would be requested to sign a team oath. Within a few days, this team had created a professional-looking certificate stating "I, _____, vow with all my professional ethics and promise to never speak ill or in a derogatory manner against another staff member." Each person signed it. At the same time, the team suggested that if there were any issues or concerns about an individual's professional behavior, they were to be brought to the attention of the leadership team and then not talked about again. In this situation it worked. The planning focus and the signed oath united the staff to work professionally in a way it had not experienced in two or three years.

PART IV

Collaborative Teams

The power of self-managing teams has been demonstrated in numerous settings. Why do they work? Quite simply, people of groups of ten to thirty can get to know one another well, can learn virtually every one else's tasks, can be gotten together with little fuss, and under enlightened leadership can readily achieve unit cohesion and esprit.

—Peters (1987, p. 302)

Team synergy calls for the team-building skills that can move a team in the direction of consensus. Teams do not just happen. There are many ways the parts can act together. Most of us have many experiences of groups of people who have no knowledge or capacity for acting together. Leadership skills and openness are required. Likewise, consensus does not just happen. People who have been trained in rugged individualism and in confrontational modes of operating cannot overnight become smooth-operating teams facile at creating consensus.

Getting people to sit around a table together does not guarantee a smooth-working team. Indeed, Blake, Mouton, and Allen (1987) refer to the potential of either "positive collectivity" or "negative collectivity." When a positive collectivity is created, the way is paved for authentic consensus. The connections and links made among individuals open up the potential for consensus. The deeper the team connection, the greater the potential for consensus.

Team synergy emerges from a skillful focus on both the external team task and the trust and nurturing among the team members. Single-minded drive toward the team task soon leads to burnout or robotic accomplishment of duties. Warmth and mutual support soon turn sterile in the vacuum of a self-serving group. Synergy is the product of deep human connections joined in accomplishing a common task.

"Valuing the differences is the essence of synergy—the mental, the emotional, the psychological differences between people" (Covey, 1990, p. 277). The heart of team synergy is discovering the value of the differences that exist in the team. When the positive value of the individual differences is embraced, then the capacity to build consensus increases. At the same time, the team cohesiveness and the team energy expand.

Operating in teams is a mode of working that is totally different from either the top-down decision-making mode chief executive officers have used or the instructional mode teachers have used. Both the teacher and the chief executive officer have been the primary focus of information in those old modes. Today, the style of the facilitator presupposes that much knowledge exists already among the workers in the organization. Calling it forth, building on it, and extending it beyond what is already known demand new skills of operating. What is at stake is effectiveness. The old modes no longer work.

Peter Senge (1990) gives us a clue to the kinds of skills needed. Some skills enable a group to get as many ideas as possible. These skills enable a group to see a variety of available options, which can be gotten out on the table relatively quickly with little or no evaluation or judgment. Once that has occurred, then the group needs methods to narrow the options down to a workable number. Finally, the group needs methods to decide which options it will go with. These are not the methods most familiar to a society accustomed to top-down decision making or confrontational battles, which the loudest or strongest individuals win.

Senge (1990) suggests that once a group is formed, it is possible to access a level of thinking that is more powerful than the individual minds. I suggest Senge is pointing to the mind of the whole group (in the best sense of the term). This "group mind" is the opposite of "group think," which refers to a group in which everyone thinks and operates the same way. The group mind as I define it is made up of many strong individual minds with distinctly independent thought. These minds are bound together for a common end. That bonding has created the group mind. Methods and tools to access this group mind can call forth creativity, alternative options, and solutions that one mind alone would have trouble generating.

Senge suggests an additional potential in a bonded team—the ability to step back from the task and reflect on what is going on in order to derive lessons and meanings. The skill to do that not only produces critical insights into the task at hand but also creates deeper bonds among the members of the team, bonds that can exponentially increase the capacity for deeper and deeper consensus.

The excitement of team accomplishment and team diversity drives the journey toward consensus. According to Covey (1990), it is critical to see excitement for the team accomplishment and interdependence as a developmental step way beyond mere dependence on other people to get your job done for you. It is a fine-tuned instrument in the process of growing and maturing. As the team members take delight in their own accomplishments and in their own experience together, the sense of team reaches new heights. The connections tighten. Challenges are looked forward to, not run away from and dreaded. Through interdependence, a powerful, effective, dynamic force is constantly being forged. "Why not collaborate? Why not get a wide variety of opinions before making a decision? This greatly improves the working environment and gives more individuals a legitimate feeling of ownership in the organization. It also gives the organization a better chance of success" (Rosberg, McGee, & Burgett, 2003, p. 10). Notice the emphasis on the working environment. A strong team has the potential of dramatically fostering an environment that motivates its members to work. This kind of environment promotes what Adams calls "inspired performance" (1986, p. 96).

When teams have reached this stage of development, each team member has come to realize that the strength of the team is built on the different gifts each person brings to it. In other words, the power of the team is in its diversity. This deep valuing of diversity, honoring of different perspectives, and welcoming of different viewpoints is precisely what enhances consensus. Differences are welcomed, even trusted. As walls of distrust come down, new levels of consensus arise. This level of team effectiveness dispels the chronic institutional dysfunctions of "fragmentation, competition, and reactiveness" (Garmston, 1997, p. 62).

When teams function well and operate out of consensus in their decision making, the result is visible accomplishment. Team members are enthusiastic about their work and ready for the next challenge. Fullan reminds us that "it is not hard work that tires us out as much as it is negative work" (2005, p. 26). Hard work that feels effective and produces visible results feeds one's drive and one's spirit. This kind of teamwork can allow each member to rejoice, "We tapped into our collective wisdom, drew on each other's courage, and in the process discovered that together we were mighty" (McEwan, 2003, p. 80).

Acting out of consensus calls for operating in a way we may find strange. Yet the evidence is in. Not only does it all work, but it is possible to have it all happen in a way that makes this very work something we want to participate in. Work has the possibility of once again generating our excitement and enthusiasm. Consensus is the vital process for making that possibility a reality.

Chapter 10

Intensifying Team Identity: Simple Things to Do

INTRODUCTION TO TEAM IDENTITY

Western society has operated in recent time with an emphasis on the individual. Responsibility and accountability occurred person by person. Now, however, particularly with the corporate world discovering the effectiveness of teamwork, collaboration is demanded in the workplace. Although individual accountability is always a critical component, communication skills and the ability to work cooperatively are sought more and more. Yet, for many of us, operating in teams comes fraught with challenges and pitfalls along with promise.

Teams increase their effectiveness as their identity is enhanced. A team is an organism—an entity, just as an individual is an organism. Affirming and nurturing this organism increases its productivity. Acknowledging the presence of teams almost needs to be overdone to successfully counter our accustomed ways of operating as individuals. Creating the bond of team dramatizes to its members another way of operating.

Consensus building is about creating trust and making connections among people. The team, by fostering a sense of identity outside the individual, inculcates a possibility of relatedness and trust that is foundational to efforts toward consensus. The more successfully teams can connect with each other and interact, the more potential there is for genuine consensus.

≈53≈

Team Member List

Teamwork is a plural process. It cannot be done by one person.

—Blake, Mouton, and Allen (1987)

Description

Listing the teams and the team members is foundational. It is a declaration of how things are going to operate. In the past, teams have been primarily advisory. In shared decision making, teams are for implementation. Some recommendations or decisions will be popular, and some will be disliked. A list of team members makes visible the mechanism now operating for recommending, deciding, and implementing.

Naming the team members gives the broader group access to what is going on. A worker might be reluctant to ask the manager about a particular issue. On the other hand, the same worker on a coffee break might talk more easily to a fellow worker on the appropriate team.

The list of team members is the new organizational chart. It may be a little oversimplified, but it can symbolize that now the recommendations, decisions, and accountability lie with the teams. In addition, it is a tool that communicates the importance of every individual to the life and success of the team.

Did You Know?

- A list of team members communicates that everyone is needed for the accomplishment of the group task.

- Keeping the list up to date communicates that teams are vital to the success of the group.

Activity: Team Member List

1. Print a list of all team members, using their full names, spelled correctly.

2. Make sure that everyone on the team receives a copy of the list.

3. Make sure the list is posted in the meeting room area and in a central area for all to see.

4. As changes occur, update the list.

5. Use the list to take attendance at the team meeting.

Hints

- The radical nature of the team member list can become apparent when the first controversial decision needs to be made. In the past, organizations have named a manager to be the one to both make a decision and take the praise or blame. The new approach suggests that recommendations come from the teams and are to be reviewed by the whole group or a representative body.
- Many managers may want to rescue their teams from controversy or even outright hostility. A much trickier role for the manager is to make sure each team has all the data necessary to make an informed decision. Then it is time for the manager to step back and allow the consequences of shared decision making—both the uplifting ones and the struggles—to unfold.

Example

When leading a planning session, it is helpful to move into implementation planning teams after doing several sessions of whole-group planning. When people prepare the entire planning document, the list of who is on which team is included. This is part of what can remain long after the workshop.

To ease into this mode of operating, some groups suggest that every person be on at least one team—of their own choosing. This approach blends elements of assignment and choice. The team list communicates to the group that shared decision making is to continue from that point on.

≈54≈

Team Name

Dependent people need others to get what they want. Independent people can get what they want through their own effort. Interdependent people combine their own efforts with the efforts of others to achieve their greatest success.

—Covey (1990)

Description

After a team has worked a short while together, choosing a team name is one way to encourage team identity. Naming the team becomes a way to assume ownership of the team, of acknowledging that each person is now part of a group accountable for a specific task. The name may be somehow related to the team task, in which case it solidifies the members in their team focus. Or the name can represent a quality or characteristic that the members want their team to embody.

Did You Know?

- The team name can remind each team member of his or her connection with the others on the team.
- The team name formally identifies this new team organism.
- The team name can communicate the team's unique gifts and personality.

Activity: Team Name

1. Clarify who the members of each team are. Make sure that everyone has been placed on a team.

2. After the teams have done some planning together so that individuals have had some initial contact with each other, have each team return to the team work space for five minutes to come up with a team name.

3. Suggest to the group that the name might come out of the particular team's assigned responsibility or out of the personalities or skills of the members.

4. After each team has chosen a name, bring all the teams back together to hear team reports.

5. Clap for or acknowledge each team name.

6. Process the activity by asking:
   a. How did your team work together to choose its name?
   b. As all these names were announced, what did you hear or what did you think about?
   c. What has happened to us through this team naming process?

Hints

- The naming process has an added impact: The whole group's coming back together and hearing the team names creates a lot of momentum and spirit.
- Finding a team name does not necessarily take a long time. Coupling the choosing of a team name with one of the other team identity activities in this section will enhance creativity.

Example

Sometimes a particular theme for the year or a theme of a recent talk inspires a team name. In one organization, the director had given a fine talk on how well geese work together as teams. During that talk, he mentioned that geese behind the lead goose often honk as a way of encouraging the leader to keep on. Sure enough, when teams met to choose their names, one team chose the name "Honkers" to symbolize how the members wanted to keep encouraging each other and all the teams in their tasks. The name is wonderfully effective because every time the team members hear it, they will remember not only their assigned task but the style they wish to use as they carry out the task.

Another team created a name out of the first two letters of each of the team members' names: Sue, Mary, Jane, and Marilyn became the SUMAJAMA team!

≈55≈

Team Flag or Symbol

The key issue is in how the parts act together—participation. It is the core issue of productivity, creativity, and satisfaction.

—Blake, Mouton, and Allen (1987)

Description

Choosing the team name in the previous activity drew on the verbal intelligence of the group. Translating the identity of the group into a visual symbol or a flag draws on the visual-spatial intelligence of the group, thus cementing its identity in an additional mode.

Once a flag or other team symbol is created, it can become a permanent part of the team meeting area. The team flag or symbol can capture visually what that team wants to be about.

It can also be a tool to remind the team members of the big picture—the reason they are carrying out very mundane daily tasks. A quick glance at the visual symbol can tie members to the original purpose or goal for their work.

Did You Know?

- A team flag or banner proudly and blatantly proclaims the greatness of the team to its fellow group members and colleagues.

- A team flag can include unique aspects of that particular team's task or focus.
- Displaying the team flag can remind people of the significance of the team's task better than words can.

Activity: Team Flag or Symbol

1. Ahead of time, gather appropriate materials to assist the teams in this activity, such as chart paper or poster board, markers, and masking tape.

2. Give each team ten or fifteen minutes to create its visual symbol or flag.

3. Tell them ahead of time to choose a reporter. (This will alert them to the need to report and remind them that each team will be "on stage.")

4. Walk around and note the progress as a way to judge how much more time may be needed on this activity.

5. During the reports, have each team remind the larger group of its team name before describing its symbol or flag.

6. Appropriately acknowledge each presentation.

7. At the conclusion of the entire presentation, enable the group to step back and process the whole experience with one or two of these questions:
   a. What was easy about this?
   b. What was hard about this?
   c. Which flags particularly caught your attention?
   d. As you look at all these flags, what message(s) are they communicating?
   e. What did you learn about your group as you did this?

Hints

- Identity does not just happen. It needs direct encouragement. Perhaps some people have never really worked on a team before. Therefore, tools to enhance identity need to be included in the overall flow of the work of the team.

- Encourage each team to be as visual as possible.
- Some teams really build on this work. It can become a genuine source of identification.

Example

When a facilitator worked with many schools from one small city, the team that came from the northern part of the city named itself the Northern Stars and among other things put stars in its symbol. A team of math and science teachers put some science and math symbols on its flag.

Some of the flags became very elaborate, almost works of art. Motivation went sky-high after the teams shared their flags and symbols.

⮹56⮹

Team Motto

The whole is greater than the sum of its parts. The team result has exceeded the sum of individual contribution; that's . . . when teamwork becomes spectacular.

—Blake, Mouton, and Allen (1987)

Description

A motto or slogan is a further piece of identification for a team. A short phrase or sentence can hold some crucial part of the team task or summarize the team's hopes and visions.

A motto or slogan is upbeat; no one writes a depressing motto. This activity provides a vehicle for affirmative team spirit to be declared. The very process of choosing a team motto helps the team focus, through the power of language, the unique essence of the team's spirit.

Did You Know?

- A team motto can capture in a few words just what that team is all about.
- A team motto, which can be remembered during times of stress and difficulty, can provide just the right motivation to keep the team going until the task is finished.
- A short, well-written team motto is hard to forget.

Activity: Team Motto

1. Have some possible mottos or slogans at your fingertips to use as examples. Have people suggest catchy
   slogans from companies or advertisements.

2. Give each team five minutes to come up with its own
   motto or slogan.

3. Have each team choose a reporter to share the motto
   with everyone.

4. After each team is finished, call on the reporters to
   share the mottos with the whole group.

5. At the end, process the experience with one or two of
   these questions:
   a. Which word or phrase do you remember?
   b. Which one(s) do you like?
   c. What are some of the important themes communi-
      cated by these mottos and slogans?

Hints

- Since a lot of the value of these team-identity activities
  is ongoing, creating ways to keep these names, flags,
  and mottos in front of everyone can further increase

their power. Everyone is encouraged and empowered by all the teams' creativity and spirit.

- As you can see, each one of these activities does not need to take a long time. In just ten minutes out of a ninety-minute meeting, you can generate a great deal of spirit and create a difference between a boring committee meeting and a lively team meeting that can actually leave people refreshed and motivated.

Example

Some national organizations created the slogan "Science matters. Math counts." That slogan will be remembered for a long time. Furthermore, it reminds us of the crucial role of science and math.

The Northern Stars team mentioned earlier created the slogan "The stars will shine." That slogan could communicate that these people intend to carry out activities that will be noticed. Another team's slogan is "Every kid's a winner with us." This communicates the hope that every student's gifts can be discovered and released.

⫷57⫸

Team Song

Only when concern for a team result is integrated with trust and mutual support among members is synergy likely to emerge.

—Blake, Mouton, and Allen (1987)

Description

In a relatively short time, you can lead a team in writing its own team song. By choosing a melody and doing a short brainstorm on the history, role, or qualities of your team, you can assemble the ingredients for a song. Tapping the creativity of the whole team can produce the words to fit the melody. The song can be just one verse, one verse and a chorus, or even several verses.

We already know that songs can communicate feelings and commitment in a way that words alone miss. A team song can tap the power of poetry and the spirit of music and infuse them into the team experience. Just as with a slogan, it is very hard to write a negative song about your team. A song can celebrate both the importance of the team task and the appreciation of the teammates for each other as they work together.

Did You Know?

- A team song can be written even if you are not good in music.

- A team song holds power to connect that plain words do not.
- When team songs are heard by others, the songs occasion great appreciation for the creativity of the team.

Activity: Team Song

1. Give people the choice of composing a song, rap, or team cheer. This activity should take about twenty minutes.

2. Brainstorm ideas and phrases that tell how the team has worked together. This is a good time to mention some of the group's recent accomplishments.

3. Then brainstorm on paper some tunes that people know well, are fairly singable, and are upbeat.

4. Once you have listed several tunes, have the group pick one to work with.

5. When the tune has been picked, work with the group to "line out" the song. Lining out a song means drawing a short line for every syllable of the words to that song.
For example,
YAN KEE DOO DLE CAME TO TOWN is seven syllables.

__ __ __ __ __ __ __

6. After you have lined the verse, ask, "How shall we start?"

7. Gradually, people will fill in the lines with words and phrases, using some of the ideas from the brainstorm and others that just occur to them.

8. Changes and revisions will be made continually.

9. When a verse is done, have the team sing it through to see how it sounds. This will create further revisions, perhaps, or inspire the team to write another verse.

10. Listening to the songs other teams have written really raises the mood of the teams.

11. As each team sings its song, applaud or recognize each team for its creativity.

12. Ask one or two processing questions at the end:
    a. What did you like about this?
    b. What insights came to you as you were writing your song?
    c. What did you discover about yourself or your team as you wrote your song?

13. Later, have the teams sing their songs or even add new verses.

Hints

- This activity works well with a group of people who have worked together for a while. You might do it two or three months after the team has been formed. It will not work with a group that feels singing is a waste of time. Many people do not like to sing or feel it is silly for a work team to engage in singing. Many cultures, however, have realized the value of a song for focusing the energies of people for work.
- When a team seems to be stuck on an issue or a problem, having the team sing its song can often break the thinking loose.

Example

A number of teachers and businesspeople worked together on "Partnership Projects" in Appleton, Wisconsin. These Partnership Projects were an effort to create business-education partnerships in Appleton. During the second conference, one part of the group created a song and another part created a story. After a time together to brainstorm what might go into both, the song group created the following to the tune of "Hey, Look Me Over":

Hey, look us over
See what we've done
We've got ideas and
It's been lots of fun.
To help our Valley grow
Businesses and schools
And parents and kids
We're all a part of
The show. . . .

AND NOW IT'S

On to the future
There's lots that we can do
Shadowing and sharing
There's always something new
Partnership Projects
have started us moving
So come let's get the job done
We're the future

WE ARE ONE!

≈58≈

Team Rituals or Rites

Life is, by nature, highly interdependent. To try to achieve maximum effectiveness through independence is like trying to play tennis with a gold club—the tool is not suited to the reality. Interdependence is a far more mature, more advanced concept.

—Covey (1990)

Description

Simple rites and rituals just emerge naturally in the life of a team. The leader may not plan for them; often they just happen. And then the wise leader lets them grow.

Sometimes it is a word, phrase, or something that happened to one of the team members that gets repeated again and again in similar team situations. All these help a team create its own identity, making it a distinct group among all the other teams.

Did You Know?

- Some of the best team rituals and rites appear naturally and unexpectedly rather than during a team session to create one.
- Team rituals and rites often emerge after a sudden team breakthrough or victory.

- Because team rituals and rites are often linked to victory or breakthrough, they can motivate the team by indirectly reminding the members of the victory and breakthrough.

Activity: Team Rituals or Rites

This activity fosters gestures, phrases, or objects that take on a unique and special role in the life of a team and help each team member claim its identity.

1. As these rituals or rites often appear without warning, there is no substitute for keeping alert for their occurrence.

2. Your very relaxed and open style as a leader-facilitator can encourage such rituals or rites to emerge.

3. If you experience a team success or a project breakthrough, you can capitalize on the sense of accomplishment or victory by asking, "What gesture or phrase could capture how we are feeling right now?" or "What gesture or phrase would congratulate us all for this job well done?"

4. Watch the dialogue. If this idea catches on, let the team try to come up with something.

5. If not, verbally congratulate the team and suggest that maybe at another time a ritual or rite might emerge.

Hints

- Some teams meet every week or two just to celebrate their victories. Maybe it is over coffee. Maybe they have breakfast together or go out for lunch.
- Rituals and rites may seem to take time away from carrying out a task. In reality they keep people's motivation and performance ability high. The wise leader is pleased when such things grow.

Example

One team has created a gesture: The members all slap their hands together in the center of the table when they have completed their task. No other team has done that. It belongs uniquely to that team and bonds the members together every time they use it.

Another team had a "cynic jar" in the center of the table. Whenever anyone made a cynical comment or cut off an idea at the start, that person deposited a nickel in the jar. The team created this rite very naturally to foster encouragement and to strengthen awareness of unhelpful and cynical comments.

Chapter 11

Increasing Supportive Connection: Things That Take Effort

INTRODUCTION TO CONNECTION

Connection has to do with the ties people on the team sense among themselves. People who feel connected can say one or more of the following sentences: "When I speak, I am understood. My ideas make sense to others on the team." "If I am having difficulty carrying something out, I can get some supportive suggestions." "When I run into an unexpected additional work assignment, I can turn to the people on the team for some concrete assistance." "I am ready to offer help to teammates when a personal issue prevents them from finishing a task." "I always check a new idea out with a member of the team." This kind of deep connecting emerges as the trust among teammates continues to grow.

A collaborative team needs not only a strong team identity but also individuals who are connected to each other, who in their work interact and interrelate with each other. They grow in knowing that they can trust their teammates. They learn to depend on each other. This sense of connection does not happen automatically and never gets much of a start in some teams.

Genuine connection thus becomes one of the critical ingredients of authentic consensus. Because genuine connection takes a while to emerge, true consensus does not happen overnight with a group pulled together for the first time. The more serious the issue needing consensus, the greater the need for some sense of connection.

≈59≈

Winning Team Story

*When people come together to form groups, each member
brings a personal set of knowledge, skills, values, and
motivations. How these interact to form a collectivity can
be positive or negative.*

—Blake, Mouton, and Allen (1987)

Description

Every individual as well as every team possesses a conscious or unconscious story. This activity creates awareness of
a team's story and enables the team to live and work with the
empowerment a winning team story brings. Specifically, this
activity guides the team to write its own story.

Marty Seldman's book *Self-Talk: The Winning Edge in Selling*
reminds us of the role of individual self-talk relative to an
individual's performance in selling, and his insight goes much
further than selling and the individual: "What we believe and
say to ourselves quickly and strongly influences our feelings and actions" (Seldman, 1986, p. 10). A team's spoken or
unspoken, written or unwritten story about itself can have a
direct impact on its own performance.

This activity makes a team's story explicit, which will
increase the team's effective performance over time by strength-
ening its sense of connection.

Did You Know?

- When the going gets rough, a winning team story reminds people of past victories and future hopes.
- A winning team story sets the present moment into a much broader picture.
- Individuals need to be reminded that they are part of a winning team even though their particular tasks might be going poorly.

Activity: Winning Team Story

1. Set out materials such as chart paper, markers, masking tape, pencil, and paper.

2. Set the stage by saying a few words about the role of winning stories. You might ask the group the following questions:
   a. What successful teams have you been a part of?
   b. What stories do you imagine these teams had about themselves that helped them win?

3. With the whole group, brainstorm ideas under each of these three areas:

THE PAST	THE PRESENT	THE FUTURE
(What has happened; our past accomplishments)	(What is going on now; our current challenges)	(Where we want to be; future victories)

4. Divide the whole group into three teams, one to work on each of the three areas.

5. Have the teams take ten to fifteen minutes to pull together a paragraph on their assigned section. You might suggest they write their paragraphs on chart paper, which will be easy to display to the whole group.

6. Have a representative from each team read the team's paragraph.

7. Applaud after the whole story has been read.

8. End with some processing questions:
   a. What words or phrases do you remember from our story?
   b. What parts of the story did you like best?
   c. What does the story communicate about what kind of team we are?
   d. What do you think we should do with this story?

Hints

- This activity can be done in conjunction with writing the team song (see Activity 57).
- You might decide to get this story printed up and distributed to everyone in the group. Every so often having this story read could remind people in a positive and indirect way why the team exists and why the members are connected to each other.

Example

A group in Wisconsin was creating business-education partnerships between local businesses and the local schools. The members of this group called the effort Partnership Projects. After the first year of implementation, the group wrote this story about its work and its role.

PROGRESS IN ACTION—NEW HORIZONS

Our Community Situation

Once upon a time, an energetic and growing city, located on the banks of the Fox River, was given the challenge of improving its stature.

The community recognized its shortcomings. Foremost in its concern were the few children not succeeding. Some of the children were not acquiring a work ethic, some were

---

(Continued)

(Continued)

deficient in basic skills, some were dropping out of school ... some weren't developing to their best potentials.

The community saw a need for a change ... a new breath of fresh air. Business and education alike saw this need and recognized that business was largely an untapped resource in the public schools. A mutual team effort was seen as a solution to benefit business, education, community, and children alike.

Our First Year's Accomplishments

One year ago the first Partnership Conference was held. From that conference needs were identified and ideas sprang forth.

It came to pass that a logo was established giving momentum to the partnership project.

Great feasts took place with gourmet luncheons. Awareness was expanded with career festivals, the updating of the tour guides, and the creation of a speakers bureau. Jobs were shadowed. Presentations were made to teachers. The National Symposium was attended and Partnership Conference II has brought visions of lasting significance to the year's work.

So it is said, so it shall be.

Our Hopes and Dreams

It is our vision to unify the small as well as the large businesses with the educational system to bring to our young people the promise of a better future. A future that includes an awareness of their own capabilities and how they may be contributing members of the society; to feel useful, productive, and most of all, needed in the community.

⚙60⚙

Leadership Rotation

The modest-sized, task-oriented, semi-autonomous, mainly self-managing team should be the basic organization building block.

—Peters (1987)

Description

All the roles necessary for leading and supporting a meeting can be rotated and shared among the team members. The up-front leader, the person who gets the room set up and ready, the person who takes notes on the meeting, the person who brings coffee or a snack, the person who cleans up after the meeting—all these roles can be named and a rotation system prepared to share these responsibilities.

Rotating jobs is a great way to train everyone to assume responsibility for various aspects of the life of the team. If, for example, the assigned facilitator-leader for a meeting does not know how methodologically to lead a portion of the meeting, this is an opportunity for that person to be trained. Anyone in the group with experience leading can be available to coach the newly assigned leader.

Some people have great difficulty with rotation. If the group can pull it off, rotation demonstrates a lateral team structure, in contrast to our traditional hierarchical ways of carrying out responsibilities.

Not only does this method train people, it also allows everyone's unique approaches and gifts to be used. Frequently, if people are not assigned to do something, they are reluctant to put themselves in a major role.

Furthermore, rotation demonstrates that the person who has traditionally been thought of as the leader is willing to set up the room, provide the refreshments, clean up, and wash the dishes. This willingness communicates in powerful ways that no one ever "graduates" out of the nitty-gritty tasks that help pull off an event.

Did You Know?

- Leadership rotation communicates the group members' trust in each other's competence.
- Leadership rotation reveals hidden talents.
- Leadership rotation continues to renew the energy of the team.

Activity: Leadership Rotation

This activity enables the team to create its own leadership rotation chart. Although one person could draw it up, creating the chart as a team activity fosters more buy-in.

1. Suggest that each person can do any role.

2. Brainstorm the various roles and tasks necessary for a meeting (e.g., room setup, leader, secretary, report writer, room cleanup, refreshments).

3. List those down the left side of a piece of chart paper.

4. List the next eight to ten meeting dates across the top.

5. Have the group decide how to fill in the slots (e.g., random rotation, sign-up).

6. Print this chart and distribute it to everyone at the next meeting.

7. Suggest that if any conflicts or difficulties arise, it is the individual's responsibility to make switches or changes.

8. Clarify who people can check with should they have any questions about how to carry out their assigned role for any given meeting.

Hints

- If certain people resist strongly, work around them. The alternation of responsibilities creates opportunities, not hard-and-fast rules.
- Another way to rotate assignments is to divide your group into subteams and assign the meetings to the subteams. If one person does not feel able to carry out a responsibility, the subteam will deal with it, either by encouraging the person to go ahead or by assigning a willing person to carry it out.
- Rotation entails some clear write-ups of the various responsibilities and how to carry them out.

Example

In large organizations, real training often happens in small teams that rotate assignments for various duties and responsibilities weekly. In an effective team, where connections are strong and positive, those who have been around a while are eager to assist new members.

In one organization, the various rotating roles included getting notices out about the coming meeting, leading an opening conversation to focus the team, facilitating the major workshop of the meeting, taking and distributing notes on the meeting, getting the room set up, and clearing the room after the meeting.

≈61≈

Icebreaker Opening Conversation

Interdependence is the paradigm of we—we can do it; we can cooperate; we can combine our talents and abilities and create something greater together.

—Covey (1990)

Description

It is helpful to begin a meeting, even if it will last only sixty to ninety minutes, with a short opening conversation. This conversation could be a whole-group conversation, or it could be a matter of asking each one to turn to the person on the right and talk through something briefly. Topics might relate to team concerns, dramatic current events, or general contemporary issues.

Most people walk into a meeting from very hectic, crowded schedules. The icebreaker opening conversation is not so much to break the ice among people who do not know each other as to enable people who do know each other to make the transition to concentrating on what the meeting is going to be about.

In addition, it provides a moment of personal, one-to-one interaction that can greatly relieve tension for people with harrying responsibilities. The opportunity to spend even a few moments sharing some ideas or experiences with others can be refreshing for all of us. The chance to get connected with the people who are in the group with them, however briefly, sets the stage for the collaboration and consensus needed as the agenda unfolds.

Did You Know?

- An icebreaker opening conversation offers the team a bridge connecting individual work time to group work time.
- An icebreaker opening conversation can allow people just the right chance to release a day's frustration and therefore put more positive energy into the team meeting.
- An icebreaker opening conversation can sometimes raise indirectly the concerns and issues that the team meeting will deal with head-on.

Activity: Icebreaker Opening Conversation

1. Review for yourself what the particular team task is for this meeting and ask yourself these questions:
   a. Is there a question or topic surrounding this task that would be appropriate to talk about?
   b. What has the mood of the group been lately? Are there crucial issues or topics that have been weighing it down? What question would allow the members a chance to explore their concerns and feelings about that topic?
   c. Is a current event drawing people's focus and energy away from the work of the group?

2. After a one-sentence introduction, pose the question and let people talk in groups of two or three for four or five minutes. Ask whether members would like to share something they talked about. (Of course, confidential information will not be repeated.)

3. Another option is to pose the question to the whole group and allow a full-group conversation from the start.

4. After seven to nine minutes, the group is ready to move on to the agenda of the meeting, and the members have genuinely arrived at the meeting and are now connected to the team.

Hints

- People are not accustomed to this kind of short conversation at the beginning of a task-oriented meeting. Consequently, when you initiate this strategy, be sure to pick safe questions that relate to your agenda.
- Over time people begin to look forward to these interactions.
- The success of this strategy depends on the leader's comfort with it and confidence in its potential for increasing team connection.

Example

The following is a list of various questions that can be used for this activity. (Ask just one question.)

1. What was the best team you have been a part of? What were the qualities that made it so?

2. What is something that has happened recently that made your day?

3. What are some things that concern you about our upcoming major event?

4. When have you had to think quickly "on your feet"?

5. Who do you know who is well organized? What are some of the qualities of a well-organized person? What are some tricks people like that use to be well organized?

6. What have you been learning about our team lately? What are some of our best qualities as a team?

7. How is _____ [name a current event] affecting your colleagues? What are some helpful ways people can respond?

During a depressing international crisis, a group divided into pairs to talk about it. When the whole group re-formed, people shared how helpless they had been feeling. When asked, "What are some helpful responses one can make in the midst of such an overwhelming crisis?" some people made some good suggestions. With the realization that they could do something, the group's mood shifted, and attention could focus on the meeting.

❧62❧

Dyad or Triad Brainstorming

When people are able to grapple with a difficult and complex problem and come out of it with something far better than could have been had without the joint effort, the emotional reaction is one of deep satisfaction.

—Blake, Mouton, and Allen (1987)

Description

Some leaders may begin a meeting by saying, "Everyone, this issue has come up. What do you think we should do about it?" or "This is my thinking on this issue. What is yours?" The ones who respond are those who have no difficulty speaking up or those who are very quick thinkers. This tends to exclude a lot of us.

Instead, after a topic has been proposed and people have had a chance to do some thinking individually, offer them an opportunity to work in groups of two and three. By providing time for people to talk things through in smaller groups, you create an opportunity for initial team connections to form and for the early stages of consensus to take shape. This means that the entire burden of creating consensus does not fall on the leader's direct interaction with the whole group. Some ideas can be either strengthened or weeded out in this dyad or triad stage.

Did You Know?

- Some people put more of themselves into a team of two or three than into a larger team.
- Dyads and triads tap the wisdom that often lies untapped in every individual's thinking.
- Some people will say things in a group of two or three that they do not feel comfortable saying in a larger group.

Activity: Dyad or Triad Brainstorming

1. State the major issue or the question that you want people to think about. You might add a sentence about its significance, such as the following:

   "Because our company is in a process of restructuring, we need to think through the best way to combine our two divisions and create a model of task realignment. What are the steps you think we need to take in this process?"

2. Share any relevant information; for example:

   "This financial report and market analysis will help you see why this step is important. We are hoping the whole process can be done in under a year."

3. Suggest that people spend three or four minutes thinking individually and writing their own responses. You might say something like the following:

   "In the next three or four minutes, jot down four or five ideas from your own thinking about the steps we need to take to combine our two divisions."

4. Ask the group to divide into miniteams of two or three to discuss the individual responses.

"In teams of two or three, discuss your responses from your individual thinking. Be ready to share your team's best five or six responses."

5. Then invite the teams to share their responses, either on chart paper for a brainstormed list or on 5 × 8 cards for a full workshop.

Hints

- Very often, I ask two or three people sitting near each other to form the dyad or triad.
- If you have been breaking up into these smaller teams many times in one workshop or meeting, then to mix up the groups somewhat, you might have people number off or choose someone from another table to work with.

Example

When working with a group of only four people, it might be tempting to skip this intermediate step of dyad or triad brainstorming and simply move from individual thinking to a whole-group discussion. Without the intermediate step, however, the discussion among the four can take twice as long as a discussion with thirty or forty using the dyad-triad step would take, and investing time in dyads or triads helps the ensuing discussion and consensus building go smoothly. Besides, four people can pair up in three different ways, providing rich possibilities for combining ideas and points of view.

∼63∼

Making the Differences Visible

And unless we value the differences in our perceptions, unless we value each other and give credence to the possibility that we're both right, that life is not always a dichotomous either/or, that there are almost always third alternatives, we will never be able to transcend the limits of that conditioning.

—Covey (1990)

Description

In a world of rapid change, people of many different perspectives, values, and traditions are often thrown together in a team with the expectation that the members of the team will know how to work in the midst of seemingly irreconcilable perspectives and approaches to handling issues. The most common response to situations like these is denial or overt conflict. Often the denial proceeds until some team members are at an impasse or a breaking point. Then, perhaps without premeditation or warning, a raging conflict ensues.

This activity suggests that teams start bridging the differences by making the various perspectives explicit. An essential assumption is that each perspective has value and is crucial to the full operation of the team. This activity uses the tool of a graphic organizer, such as a modified Venn diagram, to plot the differences. Afterward, appropriate questions can help the group members process and reflect on what they have noted.

Did You Know?

- Denial of differences intensifies their power to cause conflict.
- Becoming aware of differences helps us view them as less strange.
- Naming the gifts of various perspectives overtly reminds us how we need each perspective to make our whole team work.

Activity: Making the Differences Visible

1. If a team has been in conflict, initiate a conversation about what has been going on. Ask, "How does conflict usually emerge with us? How do we usually deal with it? What happens to our ability to get the job done when conflict continues?"

2. If the team feels that the cause of the conflict lies in the varying views on the team, suggest the team might want to look at these views directly.

3. On chart paper, draw three or four large interlocking circles, each circle representing one perspective (see the example on the next page). In the largest part of each circle, write elements of the perspective it represents. The trick will be to name these elements in objective, nonjudgmental language. When the perspectives are clarified, you might find a way to name the gifts of each perspective.

4. Once the differences have been delineated, push the group to name the ways any two perspectives are connected (the bridges between the perspectives).

5. Finally, deal with the intersection of all the perspectives. What are the points of connection among all the perspectives represented? What do these connections suggest about the strengths of our team?

6. At the conclusion of this activity, step back and ask one or more of the following questions to help the team process what has happened:

a. What observations did you make as we carried out this activity?

b. What seemed to go smoothly for us? What was difficult for us?

c. What happened to our team as we went through this activity?

d. How does this activity enable us to work with our differences?

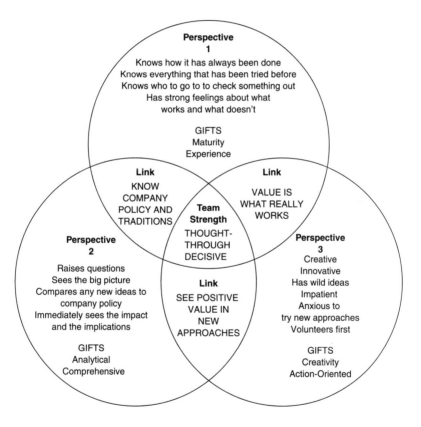

Hints

- This is an activity to use either before a conflict has exploded or after a conflict explosion has settled down. This activity will not ease a conflict just after it has exploded.

- You might at some time give a humorous name to these perspectives so that if you run into conflict again, you can refer to the conflict in a humorous way and defuse its negative power.
- Something like this can be done when dealing with a group representing two or more cultures that are unaccustomed to working together. Gaps seem wider when customs and perspectives are kept hidden. Exposing them to conversation can also expose the values lying underneath them. Often these values can be a source of real connection. In other words, look not only at the differing customs but at the reasons these customs are used. Some unfamiliar customs make a great deal of sense when their context is understood.

Example

One team was having a great deal of difficulty getting along. It hired a consultant to train the members in techniques for working through their differences. This consultant suggested the concept of different colored hats. For example, if you are speaking from a visionary, theoretical standpoint, you put on the blue hat while you speak. If you are feeling particularly angry over something, you grab the red hat before you speak. If you are raising some practical, concrete issues or problems, you put on the green hat; if you are clarifying a point, you put on a purple hat; and so on. What struck me about this was that it very specifically and ingeniously affirmed the gifts of each of those orientations. And more than that, the hats suggested that we all embody different perspectives at different times.

⁓64⁓

Team Victory Celebration

Many people have been trained and scripted into defensive and protective communications or into believing that life or other people can't be trusted.

—Covey (1990)

Description

There are many different ways to hold a team celebration. However it is done, the important thing is to do it. It can be simple or complex. It can be planned or spontaneous. The important thing is to allow celebrations to happen.

A group of twenty or thirty will celebrate from time to time. I also suggest that a smaller team of five to ten celebrate from time to time in some appropriate way. Elaborateness is not necessary. Simplicity and the fact that celebrations happen are important.

Celebrations send a message to team members that they are worthwhile and effective. By breaking the routine, celebrations sustain motivation for the long haul.

Did You Know?

- Even little celebrations feed the spirit of the team.
- Celebrations connect people in different ways than discussions and teamwork do.

- Variety in celebrations adds zest and excitement to the life of the team.

Activity: Team Victory Celebration

These are the critical elements to include in any celebration. The setting can be a regular team meeting or part of a celebrative meal.

1. A time for the teams to list their victories and accomplishments.

2. A place for the teams to list or show all their accomplishments for everyone to see.

3. A chance for each team to read its list of accomplishments.

4. An opportunity for anyone else to add to the list of any team.

5. A chance to step back and reflect on the impact of this information about victories and accomplishments. Some of these questions might be helpful:
   a. What victories surprised you?
   b. Which ones had you forgotten?
   c. Which ones particularly pleased you?
   d. Which ones were easy to accomplish? Difficult to accomplish?
   e. What new position are we in because of these accomplishments?
   f. What does this celebration tell us our next steps need to be?

Hints

- The day-to-day operation of teams makes it quite difficult to keep your attention on things that might be going well.
- A celebration could be a regular occurrence at the end of a specific time period such as a quarter or half year.

A celebration could be a spontaneous occurrence at the end of a particularly long project, or it could come at an announcement that a proposal has been accepted or that a team has just received an award.

- Celebrations are something different from the day-to-day routine.

Example

One group celebrated the end of the first three months of its plan with a potluck lunch.

One team celebrated the end of a project by going to a movie together.

A school celebrated getting off the state at-risk list by inviting the governor to come and speak.

Some companies celebrate a team's victory by the manager's or chief executive officer's taking the team to lunch.

Some companies send winning teams on a paid vacation!

One team celebrated by witnessing a new technological advance that could streamline its work.

Chapter 12

Enhancing Group Reflection: For the Committed

INTRODUCTION TO REFLECTION

Reflection is the opportunity to step back and think about what you have been doing, how you have been doing it, and what has been going on with the people you have been doing it with. Many people call it the "processing" part of a meeting or event.

Reflection is a time of connecting. It allows people an opportunity to connect what has been happening with other ideas or other experiences they have had at other times in their lives. It also gives people a chance to connect with each other through thoughts and feelings they haven't expressed before. And it provides them an opportunity to articulate matters they have been struggling with.

When these connections happen, the potential for deep consensus within a group increases exponentially. People who feel this connected can see places and possibilities for agreement that normally would go unnoticed or unimagined. Consequently, enhancing group reflection has a very deep and profound impact on the ability of a group to create and expand authentic consensus.

≈65≈

Processing Partners

Teaming is perhaps the most challenging format for skill-ful leadership work. For one thing, successful teaming rests on the capacities of individuals to form relationships that enable them to work well together.

—Lambert (2003)

Description

This activity suggests frequent use of participant pairs to enable reflection and processing of team planning or team implementation. While it doesn't need to last long, this activity encourages taking time to step back and make some sense of what has been going on.

Did You Know?

- Some people find it hard to speak up in a large group. Some people even find it hard to speak up in a group of four or five. This activity enables everyone to have a voice during team planning and teamwork.
- This activity is a great way to end a meeting or a section of a meeting and ease the transition to the next part of the meeting.

Activity: Processing Partners

1. Have all the members choose a partner, perhaps some-one they don't know very well.

2. The partners can stand or find seats somewhere in the room.

3. Pose a reflective question for the partners to talk about: What do you think is the most important decision we have made today? What pleases you about how this meeting went today? What were points of struggle that this group had today? What might you have done differently today?

4. After the partners have had a chance to talk for three or four minutes, ask three or four volunteers to report some of the things they discussed with their partner.

Hints

- If you are leading or facilitating an extended planning effort lasting a day or two, it is helpful for people to keep the same processing partner throughout the day. If the team meets regularly every week or two, have people keep the same partner for several weeks and then change partners.
- This same activity can be used within a training workshop to help people process the training.

Example

Here is a sampling of the comments after such an activity:

"This activity helped me to make sense of what just happened."

"My processing partner added some helpful expansion to my idea."

"My processing partner clarified something that was confusing to me."

"Talking to just one person helped me to relax."

"This helped me to open my mind to what was going to happen next."

∽66∼

Content Processing

When you communicate synergistically, you are simply opening your mind and heart and expressions to new possibilities, new alternatives, new options.

—Covey (1990)

Description

While Activity 65 is a processing activity for pairs, this activity is meant for a whole group. After a presentation has been made, leaders can find out what group members have absorbed by having them step back a moment for a content-processing conversation. Perhaps a video has just been shown, the group has just heard a speaker, or you asked everyone to read an article before coming to the meeting. Holding this conversation can tell you, the facilitator, what aspects of the material need to be reviewed and what has already been well absorbed. This is an opportunity for people to make the material their own by connecting it to their own thoughts and experiences.

It is also an opportunity for individuals to expand their initial comprehension of the material with the insights and connections other people have made with the information.

Did You Know?

- Content processing helps people take information presented to them and turn it into their very own information.

- Content processing helps people translate the information presented into the situations of their own lives.
- Content processing reveals to everyone the different ways other people in the group are making sense of the information presented.

Activity: Content Processing

This activity is a guided discussion on a presentation that has just been made.

1. Before the presentation, you might say a word to the group underlining the significance of the topic and alerting them to note things of interest to share afterward in a guided discussion.

2. After the presentation, pose several of the questions listed below, keeping the same basic flow.
    a. What words or phrases do you recall from the presentation? (If it is a video presentation, what objects or scenes do you remember?)
    b. What were some of the key ideas or main points in the presentation?
    c. Where did you get interested or intrigued? Where were you surprised?
    d. What points seemed difficult to grasp? With which ideas did you struggle?
    e. What aspects of the material made sense to you out of your own experience?
    f. Looking at this presentation as a whole, what were some of the most important messages communicated?
    g. What are some questions this has sparked in your mind?
    h. Who else needs to hear or see this presentation?
    i. What are some of the implications for us?

3. Allow several responses to each question before asking the next one.

4. After about fifteen minutes, move to the next item on the meeting agenda.

Hints

- Note the way the progression of questions enhances participation.
- You might be tempted to skip questions a, b, and c because they appear simple and elementary. However, beginning with these questions helps make sure that everyone has understood the objective information from the presentation.
- You might remember conversations you have had that began with questions such as e, f, or g. Some groups may have difficulty jumping into a conversation of that depth or may even jump in with perspectives that have ignored some of the basic information elicited in earlier questions. Then this conversation may end up pulling people apart rather than bringing them together.
- As with other conversations suggested in this book, it is not necessary to cover every aspect of what the question is asking before moving on. The flow of the questions has set up a reflective process, whether people respond out loud or not.

Example

Before leading a planning session for a major corporation on improving its strategies for customer service, the meeting planners showed a video made by the corporation's competitor about its customer service. Showing the ways the competitor cared for its customers certainly got everyone's attention. Then spending twenty minutes in content processing allowed people to sort out the customer service practices they thought were satisfactory from those they thought clearly needed improvement.

⤚67⤙

Meeting Processing

Getting the maximum benefits from commitment, involvement, strong initiative, good inquiry, open advocacy, effective conflict resolution, solid decision making, and extensive use of critique is what spectacular teamwork is all about.

—Blake, Mouton, and Allen (1987)

Description

No matter how little time is left, stepping back and processing a meeting is absolutely critical to helping a group see its full importance. Meeting processing can enable the participants to connect with the larger significance of the meeting and its accomplishments or decisions. Furthermore, it provides an opportunity for the meeting to end and the transition to subsequent activities or tasks to occur.

If you have had a one-hour meeting, you could spend three or four minutes processing the meeting. However, even if you have only thirty seconds, you can pose a question and get three or four responses.

Did You Know?

- Meeting processing helps people make sense of the details of a meeting.

- Meeting processing allows people to see the value of the time they have just spent together.
- People's whole impressions of a meeting can be changed positively when they hear other people's ideas about what has just happened.

Activity: Meeting Processing

This activity illustrates one way to lead a short, directed conversation immediately following a team meeting.

1. Complete all announcements and settle the next meeting time.

2. Then suggest to the group that all of you together spend two or three minutes stepping back from the meeting and "debriefing."

3. Choose two or three of these questions and allow a few answers to each one before moving to the next.
   a. What have we accomplished during our meeting today?
   b. What was helpful for you personally today?
   c. Where did you, or where did we, struggle in this meeting?
   d. What things did we do that helped us reach these accomplishments?
   e. How could we improve the way we hold a meeting?
   f. How would you tell someone else what really happened in this meeting today?

4. Close the meeting appropriately—for example, by thanking everyone for their participation.

Hints

- There are many ways of stepping back and processing. The trick is creating variety so that people do not tire of this step.

- The length of time spent processing is not as crucial as honoring the dynamic of processing.
- In time, you might be able to get your group to reflect on the importance of these very processing questions.

Example

A teacher had created a list of twenty-five possible processing questions. When it came time to process a session, she had a wealth of questions at her fingertips. Some of her questions, with a few modifications, are included below.

How easy or difficult was it for us to get started? Why?

How much of our meeting was on track? Off track? What does that tell us?

What has this meeting reminded you of?

Describe the mental and physical activities that took place during our meeting. At what moments did you feel most anxious or stressed?

What factors seem to affect the quality of our meeting?

What is the next stage in the development of meetings that work?

In a lighter vein, a facilitator could ask, "If we were to set this meeting to music, what kind of music might it be?" Some responses this question has elicited appear below.

"I'd set it to jazz because some of the parts were confusing and then it came together."
"I'd set it to symphony music because everything was harmonious."
"I'd set it to rock and roll because it was lively and fun."

⇜68⇝

Teamwork Processing

You begin with the belief that parties involved will gain more insight, and that the excitement of that mutual learning and insight will create a momentum toward more and more insights, learnings, and growth.

—Covey (1990)

Description

When people are first learning to work together in a team, it may be useful from time to time to reflect on how well the teams are operating. This activity can give teams clues as to how to improve their work together. With the heavy emphasis our culture has given to individualism, it is important to find ways to smooth out and encourage the team formation process.

Another time this conversation might be useful is when a team seems to be having problems working. This activity could provide an opportunity for the team to diagnose some of its issues or problems, thereby giving it a chance to create its own solutions.

Did You Know?

- A well-functioning team does not just happen—it takes hard work.

- Teamwork processing can help a team make its own adjustments in order to perform more effectively.
- The more a team processes its operations, the more skill and sophistication it will have to process its current situation as well as its next phases of growth.

Activity: Teamwork Processing

This activity suggests that every few meetings a team leader offer some appropriate ways for team members to reflect on how the teamwork is going. The questions in this activity focus on the team itself.

1. Complete all announcements, including the date and time of the next meeting.

2. Then suggest that the group spend four or five minutes checking to see how its teamwork is progressing.

3. Choosing several of the following questions, lead a directed conversation.
   a. What were some of our team's accomplishments today?
   b. What are some things our team did today that displayed helpful teamwork?
   c. What are some things our team did that enabled the task to get done today?
   d. What did you appreciate about the work of our team today?
   e. How did our team work through things that first appeared as blocks to our teamwork?
   f. What are some things our team could do differently in our approach to a task or our work as a team?
   g. What has our team taught you about what genuine teamwork is all about?

4. If the team wants to spend time on a concern or issue, follow the team's lead. Try to guide the team to a resolution or concrete decision if that seems possible in

the short time you have. Otherwise, suggest spending more time on the issue at a succeeding team meeting.

5. Close the conversation and the meeting appropriately.

Hints

- Obviously this is not a conversation you hold every time a team meets. After the group has met a few times, it might be helpful. It might also be helpful at the end of a time period, such as a quarter or semester. The key is using methods that help the team figure out on its own how to improve its workings and how to appreciate what it is doing well. It is helpful to hold this kind of conversation long before an explosive blow-up. This conversation is better as a preventive strategy than as a reparative strategy.
- For your regular meetings, one processing question may be all you have time for.
- In addition to opportunities for processing and reflection, some teams may need some concrete suggestions to help them build skills in conflict resolution, attentive listening, and so on.

Example

When a facilitator was responsible for a team engaged in a highly complex project with which few had any previous experience, he found it necessary to hold these conversations frequently. These conversations taught him several things. First, he got clues about how much confidence the team members had in the team's ability to get the job done. Second, he was able to discern who was working well with whom and who was not working well with whom. Third, he could tell what tasks needed to be altered or whose assignments needed to be shifted to enable the work to get done. By the end of the project, the team was operating as a cohesive and confident unit.

☙69☙

Logs or Journals

Most of the self-improvement material puts independence on a pedestal, as though communication, teamwork, and cooperation were lesser values.

—Covey (1990)

Description

Another way to bring forth the processing dynamic is by using logs or journals. In other words, you could decide to conclude some team meetings with three or four minutes of writing in a log or a journal instead of holding a processing conversation out loud. You could provide journals or paper for people to put into journals later. Logs or journals may not work for every group. This activity also suggests indirectly, by the way, that a log or a journal is a helpful way for individuals to step back and reflect on personal life issues.

Did You Know?

- In a way that conversations do not, an opportunity to write allows some people to organize their thoughts.
- Writing encourages people to express thoughts and feelings they might never say out loud.
- Logs and journals can be a tool for mental refreshment.

Activity: Logs or Journals

This activity provides a few minutes for people to write about things they are learning or experiencing in the work of the team.

1. Say a few words about the importance of writing and of stepping back to look at what you are experiencing.

2. Provide team members with blank paper or a form with some questions to guide their thinking.

3. Suggest team members spend four or five minutes writing.

4. Before closing, ask if one or two people might read one or two of the sentences they have written.

5. Thank everyone and close the meeting.

Hints

- Some people begin a log or journal and adhere to it quite regularly. Others begin it for a while, break off, and begin again. It is crucial to avoid making journaling into a rule or a law. Logs and journals can be helpful activities. They are not meant to be kept just for their own sake.
- Some people may find it helpful to put only pictures or images in their journals.
- After people have written in their journals, I often ask if two or three people would share a sentence or two they have written. In addition to the individual impact this activity has, some extremely powerful reflections have been shared in this way.

Example

Some people who organized a conference for school principals decided that this kind of reflective activity was so important that they bought each principal a small blank book to use as a log or journal. Then once or twice each day of the conference, they provided time for the principals to write in the books.

If you use this activity over the course of a meeting lasting several days, you may also want to provide a way for members to return to something they wrote in their journal near the beginning of the event and see what additional ideas, insights, or reflections occur to them.

∾70∾

Career Motivation Conversation

Interdependence is a choice only independent people can make. Dependent people cannot choose to become inter-dependent. They don't have the character to do it; they don't own enough of themselves.

—Covey (1990)

Description

This activity helps group members talk together about their deep and profound motivations for doing what they are doing. In the rush of daily tasks, these matters are hard to talk about and at times, especially in the midst of crises, difficult to remember. A conversation that can help people articulate the motivations behind their career decisions feeds the spirits of everyone present.

Although this conversation is not an antidote to total group cynicism, it can be a booster in the midst of temporary group discouragement.

Did You Know?

- Human beings need constant reminders of the deep reasons they have chosen their careers.
- The day-to-day grind quickly focuses people away from the deeper significance of their careers.
- Career-motivating conversations can feed the human spirit.

Activity: Career Motivation Conversation

This guided discussion will take about fifteen or twenty minutes and provides people an opportunity to talk about some of their deeper career motivations. Use it with a team that has been meeting a while. You might introduce a full planning session with this conversation.

1. Begin with some easy questions.
   a. How long have all of you been at this work? Let's go around the room and hear the number of years from each person.
   b. Who has been doing this the longest? The shortest?
   c. What roles or assignments have you enjoyed the most? Why?
   d. What roles or assignments have you enjoyed the least? Why?

2. Then shift to some more-serious questions.
   a. In what moments or occasions have you been tempted to throw in the towel and do something else?
   b. In those times, what have you told yourself or what reminders have you given yourself that have kept you returning to this work?
   c. What word of advice would you like to pass on to those who are just beginning this kind of career?

3. Two or three profound answers to either 2b or 2c would be great. In any case, find a way to close smoothly, thanking people for sharing their thoughts.

Hints

- While people are mentioning the number of years they have been doing this work, you might assign someone to write down these numbers and add them up. It is impressive to hear the total number of years a group has spent engaged in the members' careers.

- Although this is a very serious conversation, there can be moments of laughter to help people deal with the intensity of the responses.
- People are interested in hearing about times when their colleagues wanted to quit and give up. They want to hear what has kept people returning to their jobs.
- Deciding the right moment for a group to experience this conversation is one of the most difficult aspects of this activity.

Example

A facilitator met with a team that had been meeting a lot of opposition to its work. It had met frequently, created lots of plans, and had actually had several successes, but it was not experiencing a lot of external support.

Out of the blue, one of the team members asked, "Why do you suppose we keep doing this?" The facilitator had not planned this activity for this group at this particular moment, but here it was. She stopped leading the meeting and listened to the comments, some of which follow.

"I do this because I enjoy planning new things."
". . . because I appreciate working with other people."
". . . because I want to make a difference."
". . . because I believe our community needs it."
". . . because the future is depending on efforts like mine."

In a few moments, people became aware of the big picture once again. It was as if they had been refreshed and were ready to work.

Conclusion

By now, the truth is out. Consensus is a long, careful process. There are some things you can do right now to move your group toward consensus. However, your skill as a leader is called on to decide what your group can come to a consensus about. There are some things you can ask people to do their first day on the job. There are other things you would not ask them to do until they have been on the job for a year. Some victories can happen right away, and they should be celebrated. With patience, deeper and more complicated points of consensus can be reached.

It may also be clear that on the road to consensus, conflicts are inevitable. Even with the most skilled facilitation and the most careful of processes, conflicts will emerge. Though it may be hard to believe this when a group seems to be flying apart at the seams, a conflict can be an opportunity. A conflict may be a sign that your team is deepening or expanding its vision. In this way, conflicts can point the way to a larger, more comprehensive vision.

I have just two messages in closing. In the midst of the journey to consensus, one of your jobs as leader is to continue helping to make the thinking of the group visible. Groups often get derailed when they forget or ignore the thinking they have done so far and the thinking they are doing at the moment. That is why writing things on chart paper or cards has been emphasized in this book. It is also why I suggest that you do your own writing about how things are going, continually reflecting on how things can be improved and how doing something a little differently might help your group have a breakthrough. Your own log of your group's victories and turning points can remind you how far the group has come.

The second message is a reminder of the crucial role of your teams. The more you encourage the teams, and the more you offer them responsibility and trust, the more opportunities they will have to show their strength and creativity. This shift allows you to be more of a coach and facilitator than a manager.

I welcome hearing from you about what is working, what is not working, how you have improved on some of the suggestions in this book, and finally, how you have created something entirely new, perhaps sparked by some of the material here.

Bibliography

Adams, J. D. (Ed.). (1984). *Transforming work: A collection of organizational transformation readings*. Alexandria, VA: Miles River Press.

Adams, J. D. (Ed.). (1986). *Transforming leadership: From vision to results*. Alexandria, VA: Miles River Press.

Axelrod, R. (1984). *The evolution of cooperation*. New York: Basic Books.

Baker, P. J., Curtis, D., & Beneson, W. (1991). *Collaborative opportunities to build better schools*. Normal, IL: Illinois Association for Supervision and Curriculum Development.

Baldwin, B. A. (1993, January). The morale fiber. *USAir Magazine*, 16–20.

Bens, I. (1999). *Facilitation at a glance*. Goal/QPC (1-800-643-4316).

Blake, R. R., Mouton, J. S., & Allen, R. L. (1987). *Spectacular teamwork: How to develop the leadership skills for team success*. New York: John Wiley.

Bolman, L. G., & Deal, T. E. (2002). *Reframing the path to school leadership*. Thousand Oaks, CA: Corwin Press.

Bolton, R. (1979). *People skills: How to assert yourself, listen to others, and resolve conflicts*. Englewood Cliffs, NJ: Prentice Hall.

Boulding, K. (1975). *The image*. Ann Arbor, MI: University of Michigan Press.

Buckingham, M., & Coffman, C. (1999). *First, break all the rules*. New York: Simon & Schuster.

Caine, R., & Caine, G. (1997). *Education on the edge of possibility*. Alexandria, VA: Association for Supervision and Curriculum Development.

Costa, A.L. (1991). *The school as a home for the mind*. Palatine, IL: IRI/Skylight Publishing.

Covey, S. R. (1990). *The 7 habits of highly effective people: Powerful lessons in personal change*. New York: Simon & Schuster.

Dickman, M. H., & Stanford-Blair, N. (2002). *Connecting leadership to the brain*. Thousand Oaks, CA: Corwin Press.

Dressler, L. (2004). *The consensus pocket guide: How to achieve high-commitment decisions*. Boulder, CO: Blue Wing Consulting.

Fogarty, R., & Bellanca, J. (1989). *Patterns for thinking: Patterns for transfer*. Palatine, IL: IRI/Skylight Publishing.

Fullan, M. (2003). *The moral imperative of school leadership*. Thousand Oaks, CA: Corwin Press.

Fullan, M. (2005). *Leadership and sustainability*. Thousand Oaks, CA: Corwin Press.

Gardner, H. (1983). *Frames of mind: The theory of multiple intelligences*. New York: HarperCollins.

Gardner, H. (1995). *Leading minds: An anatomy of leadership*. New York: Basic Books.

Gardner, H. (1999). *Intelligence reframed.* New York: Basic Books.

Garmston, R. (1997). *The presenter's fieldbook: A practical guide.* Norwood, MA: Christopher-Gordon.

Gerstein, A., & Reagan, J. (1986). *Win-win: Approaches to conflict resolution.* Salt Lake City, UT: Gibbs M. Smith.

Glickman, C. D. (2002). *Leadership for learning: How to help teachers succeed.* Alexandria, VA: Association for Supervision and Curriculum Development.

GOAL/QPC. (1995). *The team memory jogger.* Madison, WI: Oriel.

Hargreaves, A., & Fink, D. (2004). The seven principles of sustainable leadership. *Educational Leadership, 61,* 8–13.

Institute of Cultural Affairs. (1973). *5th City Preschooling Institute: An experiment in early education.* Chicago: Author.

Institute of Cultural Affairs. (1981). Imaginal training methods. *Image: A Journal on the Human Factor.* Chicago: Author.

Johnson, D. W., & Johnson, R. T. (1988, May). Critical thinking through structured controversy. *Educational Leadership,* 58–64.

Kaner, S. (1996). *Facilitator's guide to participatory decision-making.* Gabriola Island, BC: New Society Publishers/Canada.

Lambert, L. (2003). *Leadership capacity for lasting school improvement.* Alexandria, VA: Association of Supervision and Curriculum Development.

Lazear, D. (1999). *Eight ways of knowing: Teaching for multiple intelligences* (3rd ed.). Arlington Heights, IL: Skylight Training and Publishing.

Lazear, D. (2003). *Eight ways of teaching: The artistry of teaching with multiple intelligences* (4th ed.). Glenview, IL: Pearson Education.

Lindsay, W. M., Curtis, R. K., & Manning, G. E. (1989, June). A participative management primer. *Journal for Quality and Participation,* 78–84.

Lipset, S. M. (1985). *Consensus and conflict: Essays in political sociology.* New Brunswick, NJ: Transaction Books.

Mansbridge, J. J. (Ed.). (1990). *Beyond self-interest.* Chicago: University of Chicago Press.

McEwan, E. K. (2003). *10 traits of highly effective principals.* Thousand Oaks, CA: Corwin Press.

Naisbitt, J. (1982). *Megatrends.* New York: Warner.

Owen, H. (1987). *Spirit: Transformation and development in organizations.* Potomac, MD: Abbott.

Partridge, P. H. (1971). *Consent & consensus.* New York: Praeger.

Peters, T. (1987). *Thriving on chaos: Handbook for a management revolution.* New York: Alfred A. Knopf.

Portin, B. (2004). The roles that principals play. *Educational leadership, 61,* 14–18.

Rosberg, J., McGee, M., & Burgett, J. (2003). *What every superintendent and principal needs to know.* Santa Maria, CA: Education Communication Unlimited.

Russell, P. (1983). *The global brain.* Los Angeles: J. P. Tarcher.

Scearce, C. (1992). *100 ways to build teams.* Palatine, IL: IRI/Skylight Publishing.

Schwarz, R. (2002). *The skilled facilitator.* San Francisco: Jossey-Bass.

Seldman, M. (1986). *Self-talk: The winning edge in selling.* Granville, OH: Performance Systems Press.

Senge, P. M. (1990). *The fifth discipline: The art and practice of the learning organization.* New York: Doubleday Currency.

Sher, B., & Gottlieb, A. (1989). *Teamworks! Building support groups that guarantee success.* New York: Warner Books.

Shields, C. M. (2004). Creating a community of difference. *Educational leadership, 61,* 38–41.

Sizer, T. R. (1991, May). No pain, no gain. *Educational Leadership,* 32–34.

Sparks, D. (2001). *Conversations that matter.* Oxford, OH: National Staff Development Council.

Spencer, L. J. (1989). *Winning through participation.* Dubuque, IA: Kendall/Hunt.

Stanfield, R. B. (2000). *The courage to lead.* Gabriola Island, BC: New Society.

Stanfield, R. B. (2002). *The workshop book.* Gabriola Island, BC: New Society.

Thompson, B. L. (1991, June). Negotiation training: Win-win or what? *Training,* 31–35.

Thompson, S. (2004). Leading from the eye of the storm. *Educational Leadership, 61,* 60–63.

Townsend, P. L., & Gebhardt, J. E. (1989, June). Try continuous involvement improvement. *Journal for Quality and Participation,* 18–21.

Troxel, J. P. (Ed.). (1993). *Participation works: Business cases from around the world.* Alexandria, VA: Miles River Press.

Umpleby, S. A. (1983). A group process approach to organizational change. In H. Wedde (Ed.), *Adequate modeling of systems* (pp. 116–125). New York: Springer-Verlag.

Umpleby, S. A. (1991). Methods for making social organizations adaptive. In G. De Zeeuw & R. Glanville (Eds.), *Collective support systems and their users* (pp. 155–162). Amsterdam, The Netherlands: Thesis.

Weaver, R. G., & Farrell, J. D. (1997). *Managers as facilitators.* San Francisco: Berrett-Koehler.

Williams, R. B. (1997). *Twelve roles of facilitators for school change.* Arlington Heights, IL: IRI/SkyLight Training and Publishing.

Wynn, R., & Guditus, C. W. (1984). *Team management: Leadership by consensus.* Columbus, OH: Charles E. Merrill.

Zenger, J. H. (1985, December). Leadership: Management's better half. *Training,* 44–53.

Zmuda, A., Kuklis, R., & Kline, E. (2004). *Transforming schools: Creating a culture of continuous improvement.* Alexandria, VA: Association of Supervision and Curriculum Development.

Index

**CORWIN
PRESS**

The Corwin Press logo—a raven striding across an open book—represents the union of courage and learning. Corwin Press is committed to improving education for all learners by publishing books and other professional development resources for those serving the field of PreK–12 education. By providing practical, hands-on materials, Corwin Press continues to carry out the promise of its motto: **"Helping Educators Do Their Work Better."**